How to Draw A Leprechaun

A ST. PATRICK'S DAY CHARM FOR KIDS

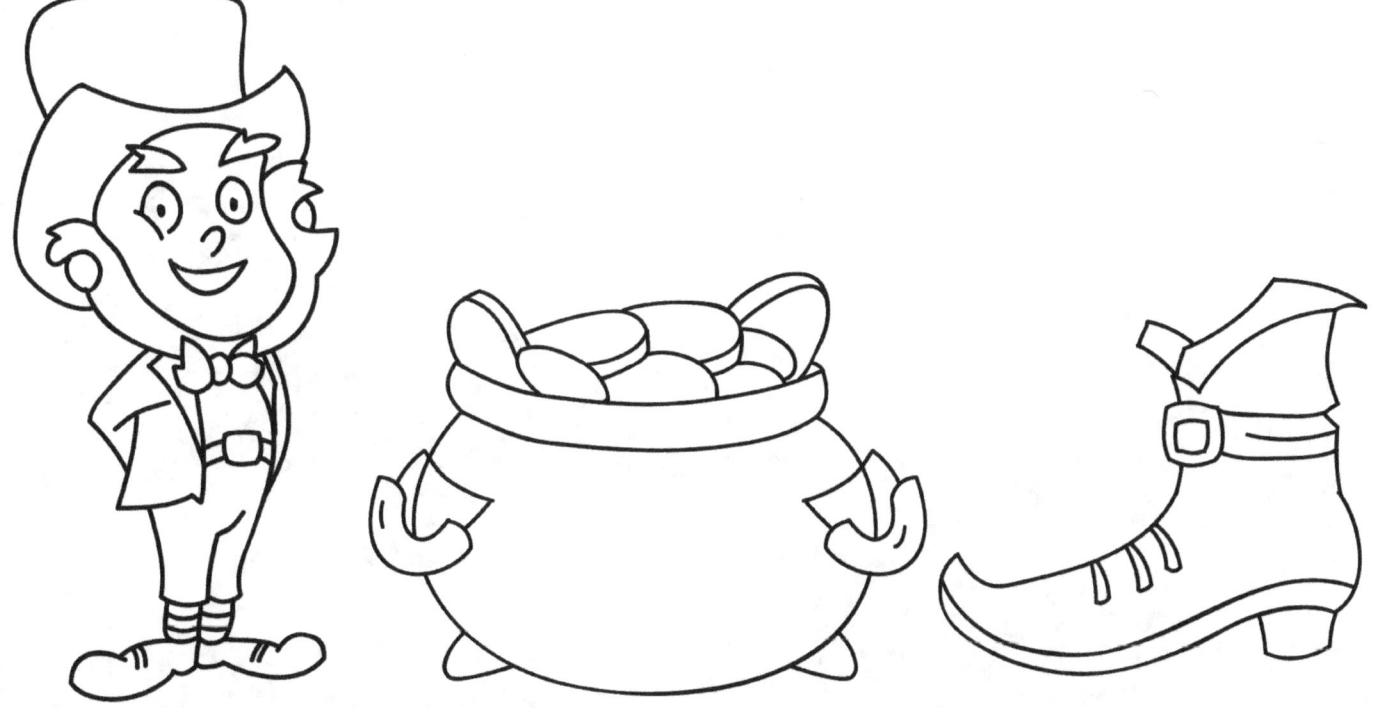

THIS BOOK BELONGS TO:

_____

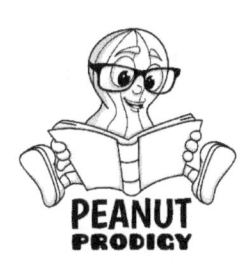

THINK YOU HAVE WHAT IT TAKES TO WIN OUR DRAWING CONTEST ?

We want you to draw your favorite picture from the book and send it into our Young Artists Drawing!

Please have your parents email us your illustration and we will select an entry to win our fully equipt art case every other month!

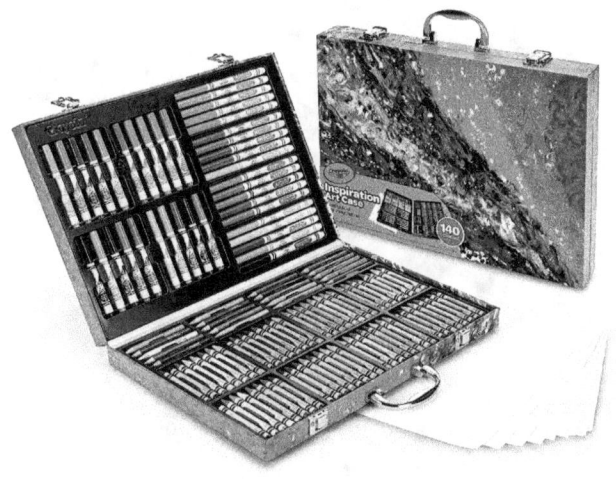

Email us your picture to:

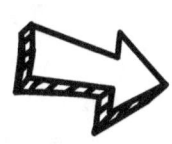 peanutprodigypublishing@gmail.com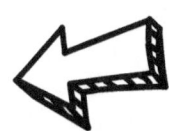

If you enjoyed this book as much as we do, please also leave us a review on Amazon. Your support is what keeps us going!

Happy Drawing!

–Peanut Prodigy Team

P.S. Even if you don't win, your entry will be put into a random drawing for a $50 Amazon Gift Card

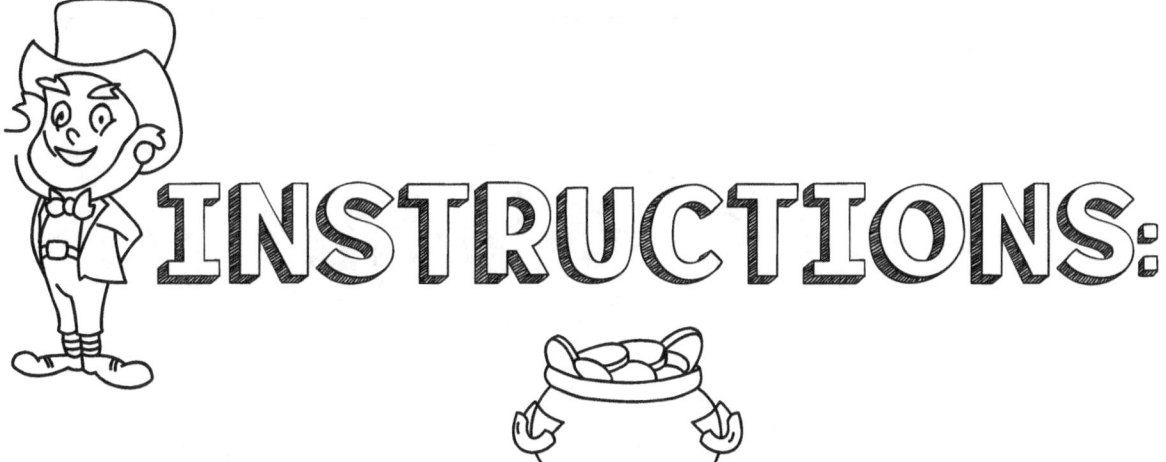

INSTRUCTIONS:

- Get ready to draw! Grab a pencil or a pen to get started.

- On the right side of the book, carefully imitate the drawings on the left side, step-by-step.

- Bring your picture to life with beautiful colors using markers, crayons, colored pencils, or watercolor paint!

- Keep your picture or give it to someone you love!

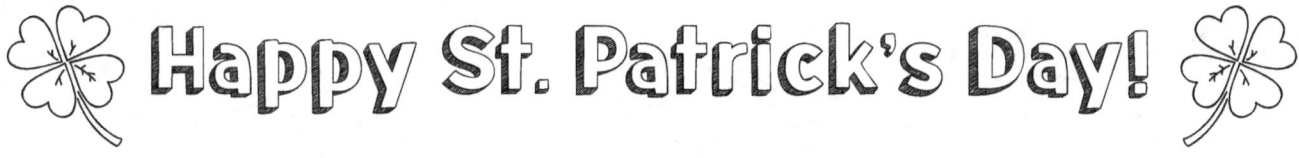

Happy St. Patrick's Day!

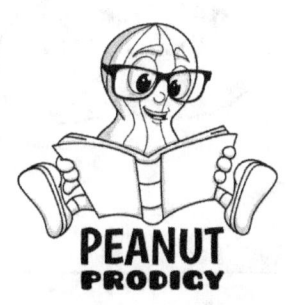

PEANUT PRODIGY

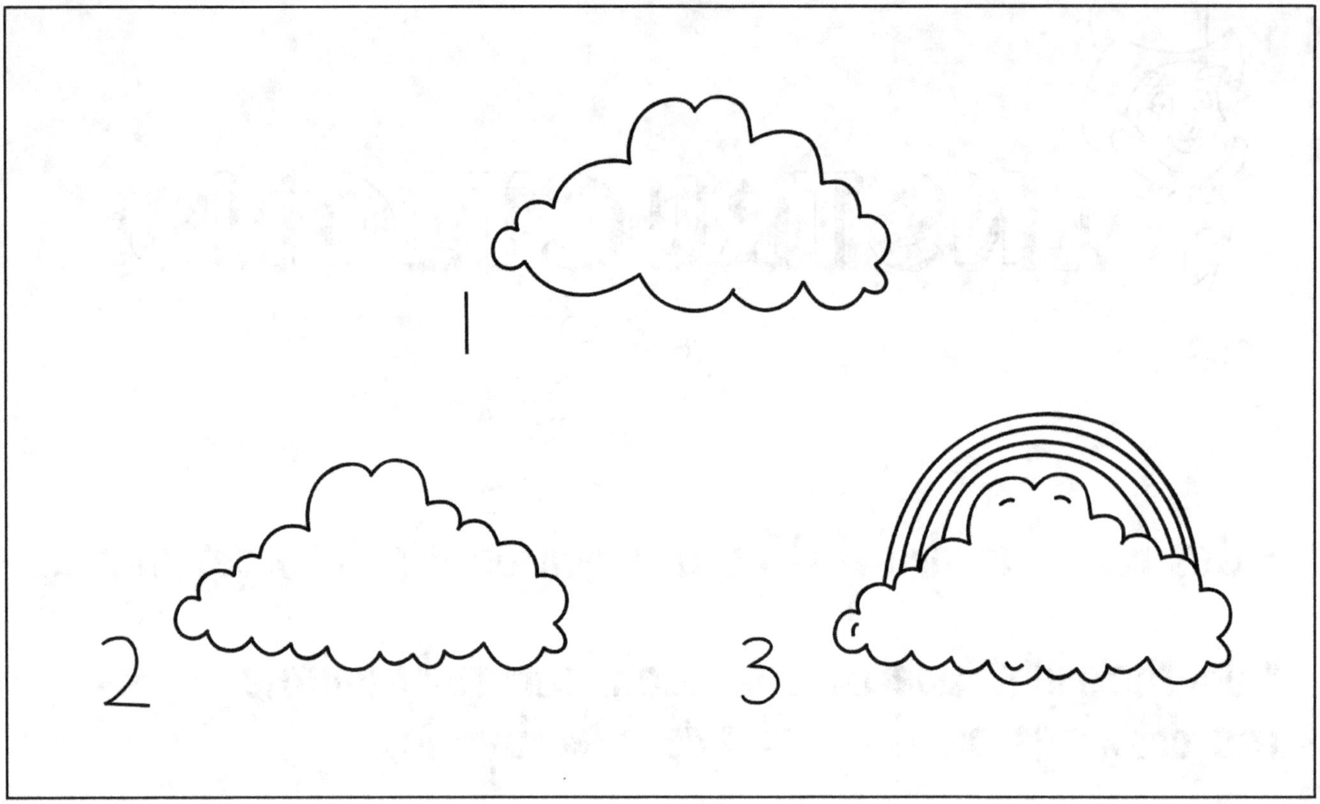

1

2

3

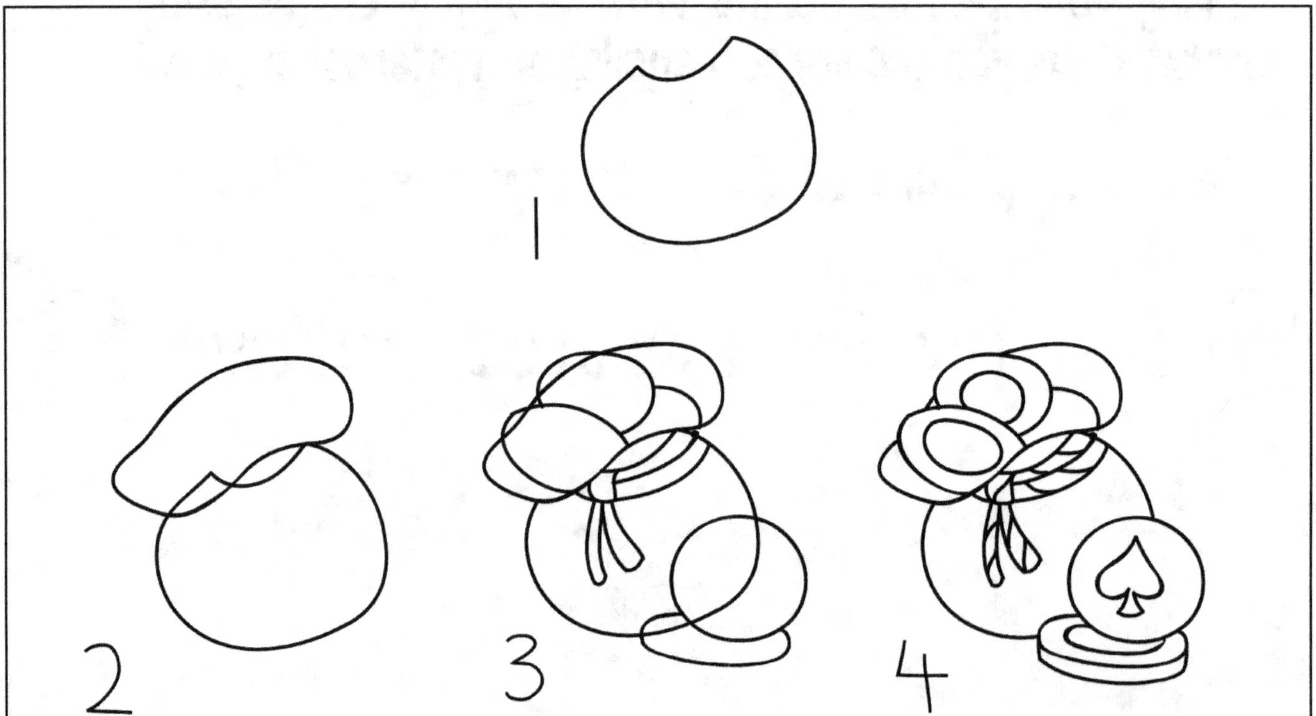

1

2

3

4

your turn to draw

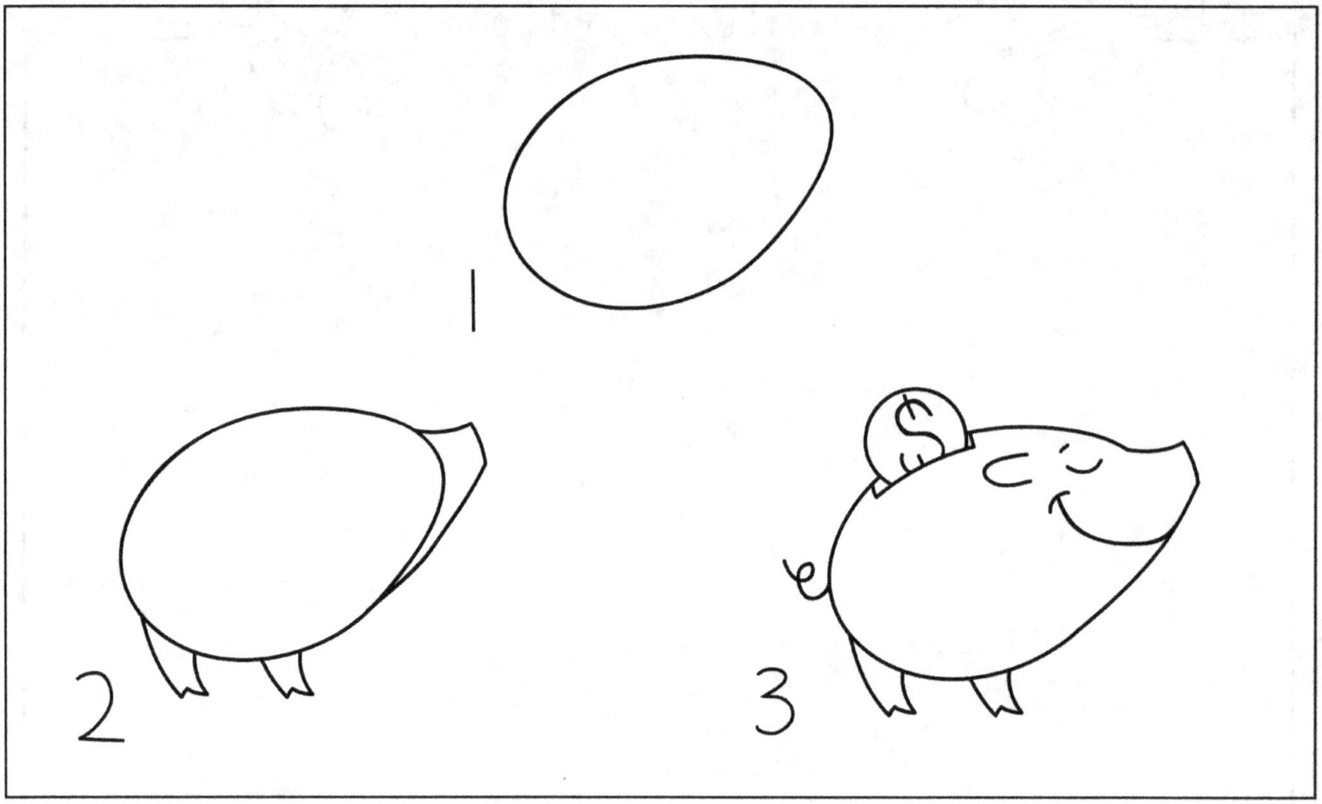

1

2

3

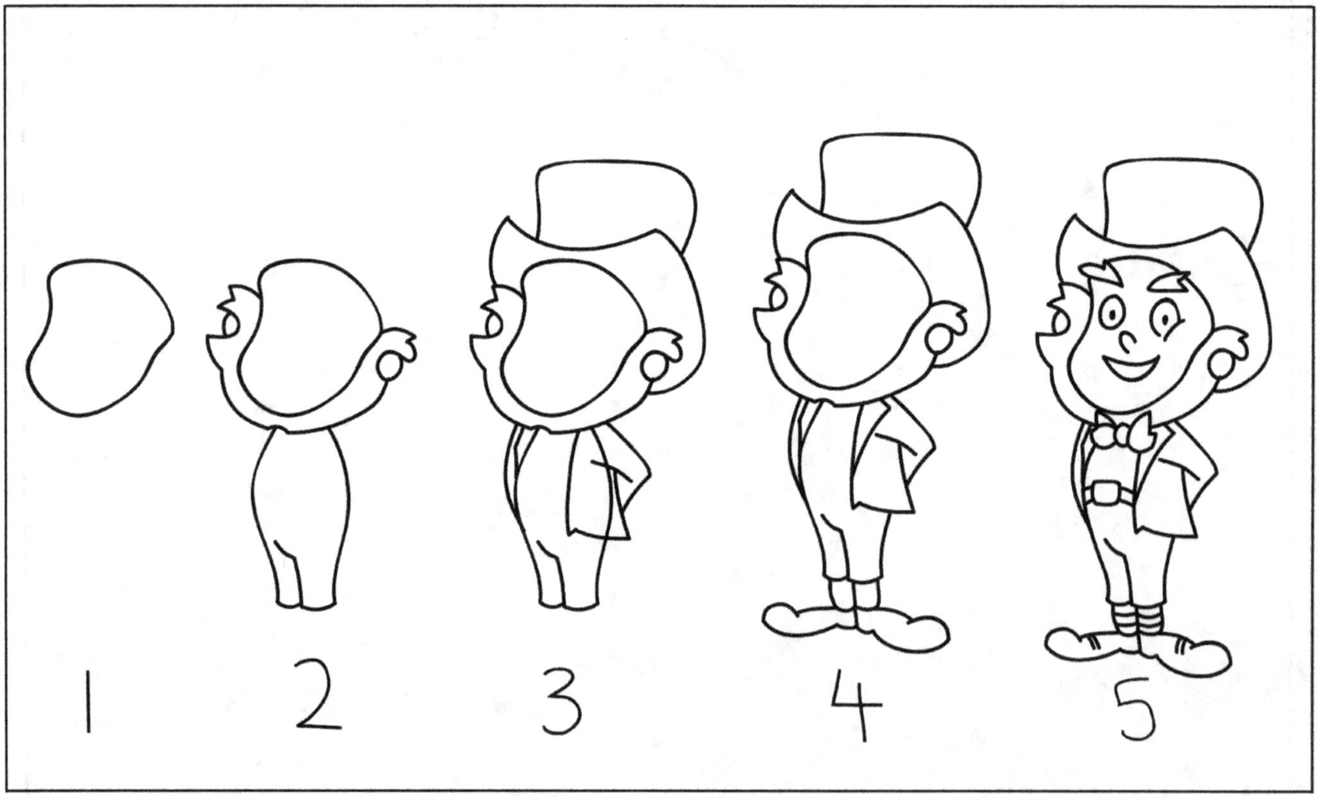

1   2   3   4   5

your turn to draw

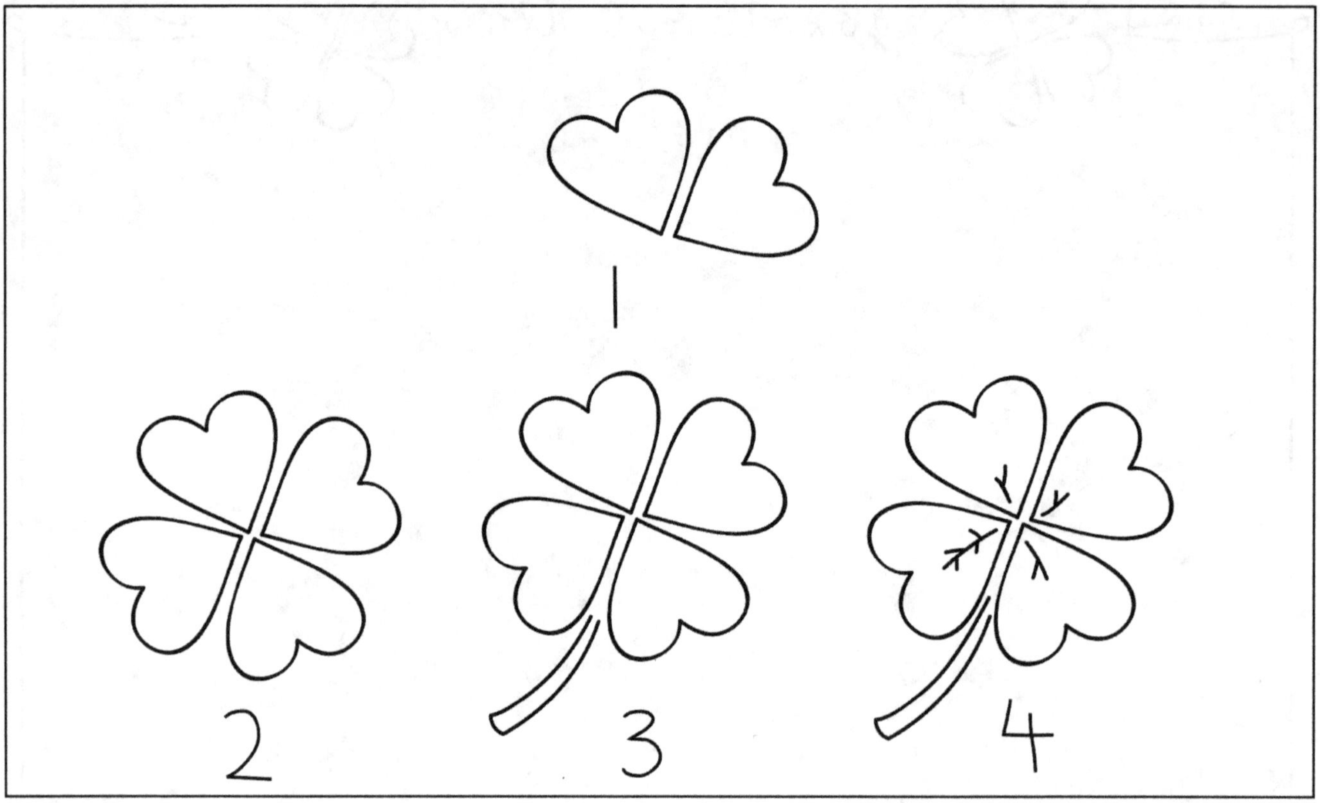

1

2   3   4

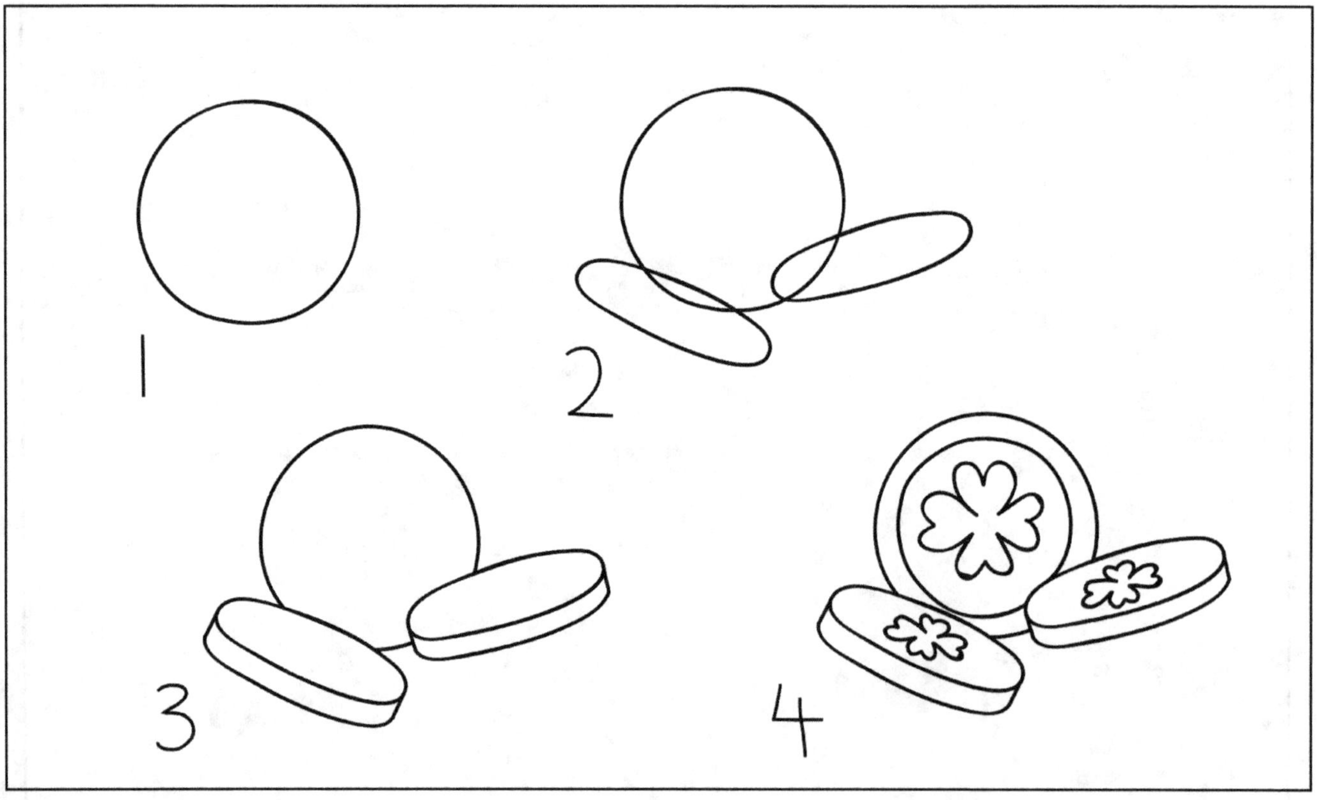

1   2

3   4

your turn to draw

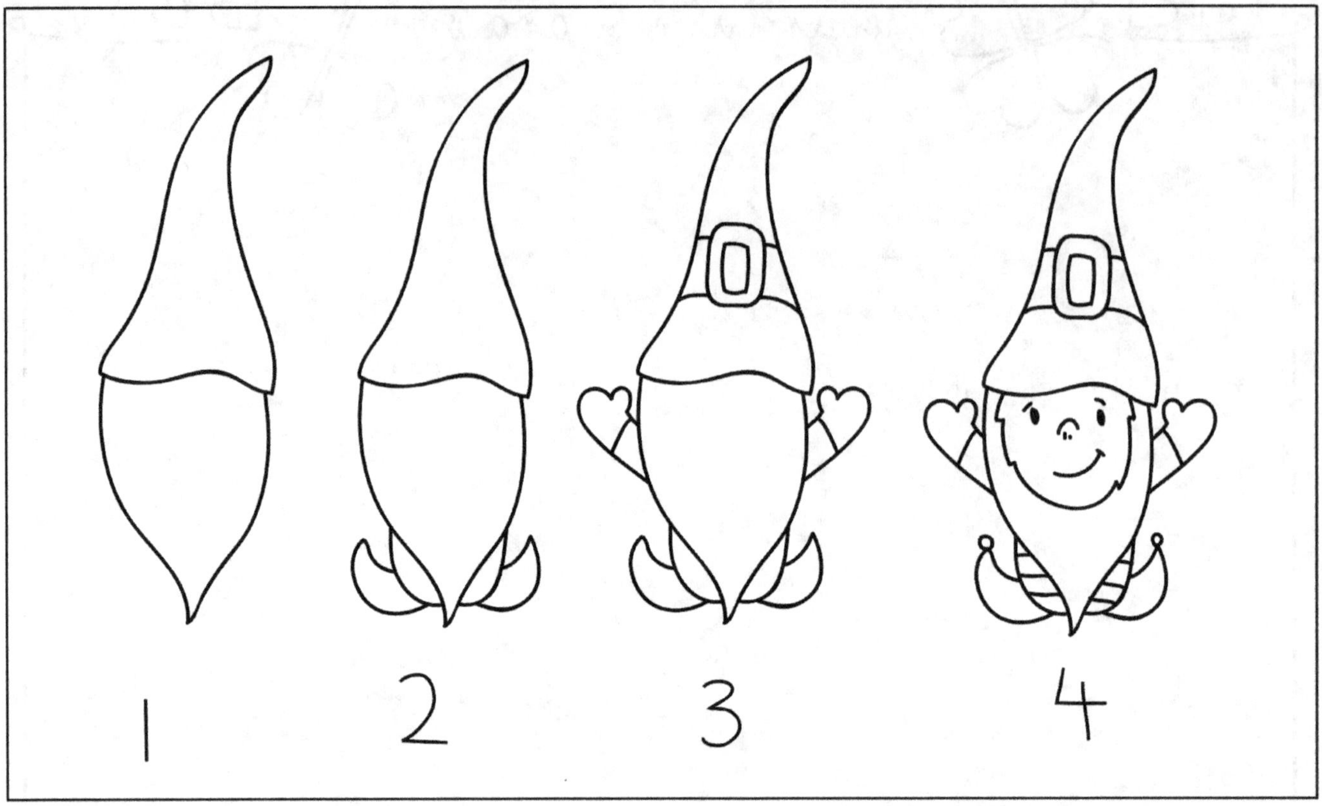

1   2   3   4

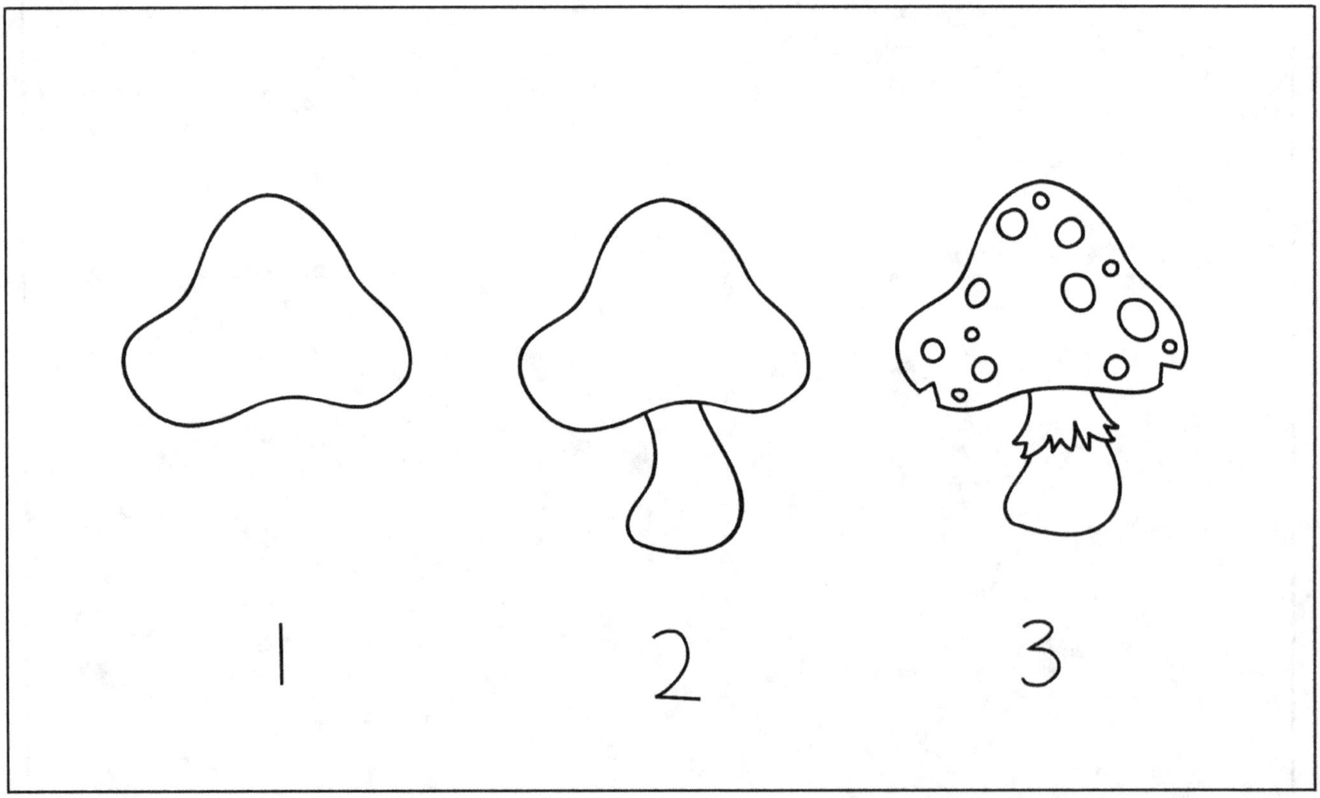

1   2   3

your turn to draw

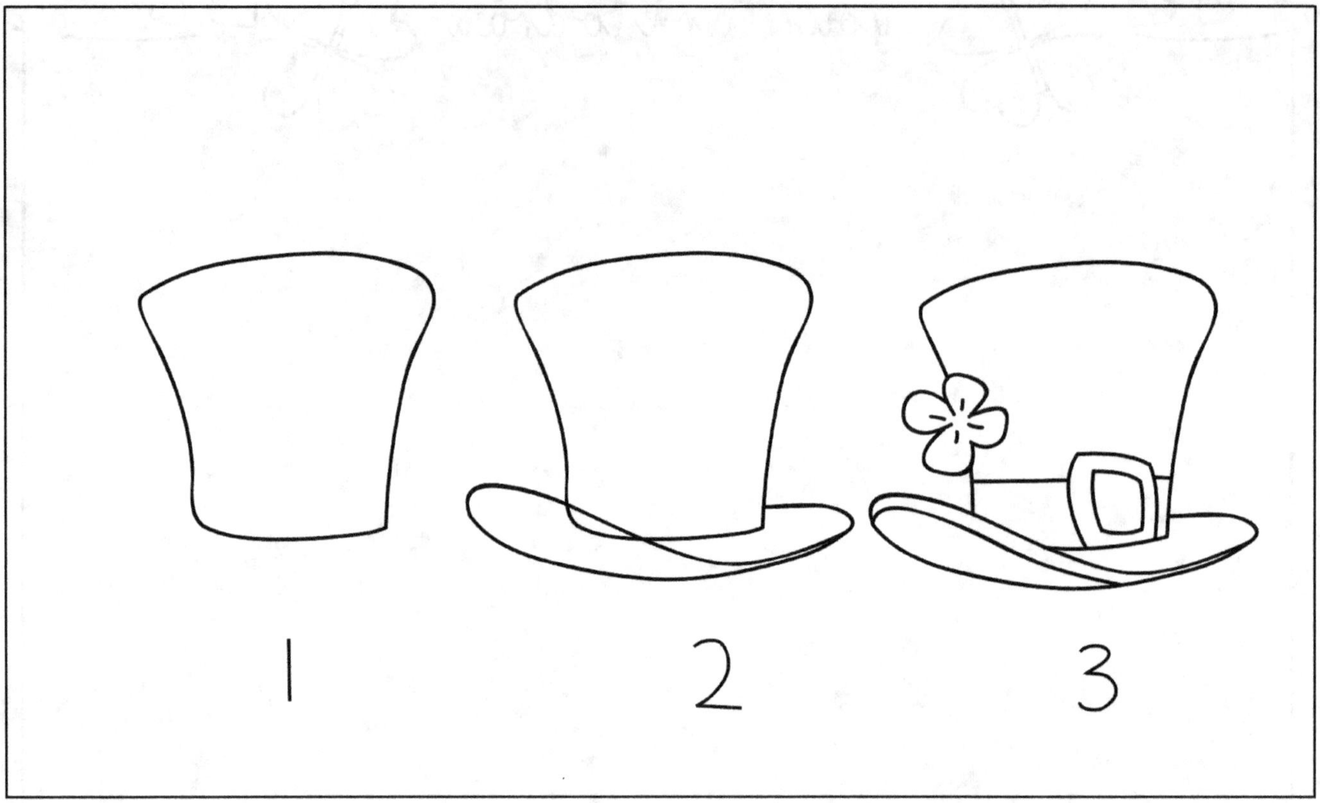

1   2   3

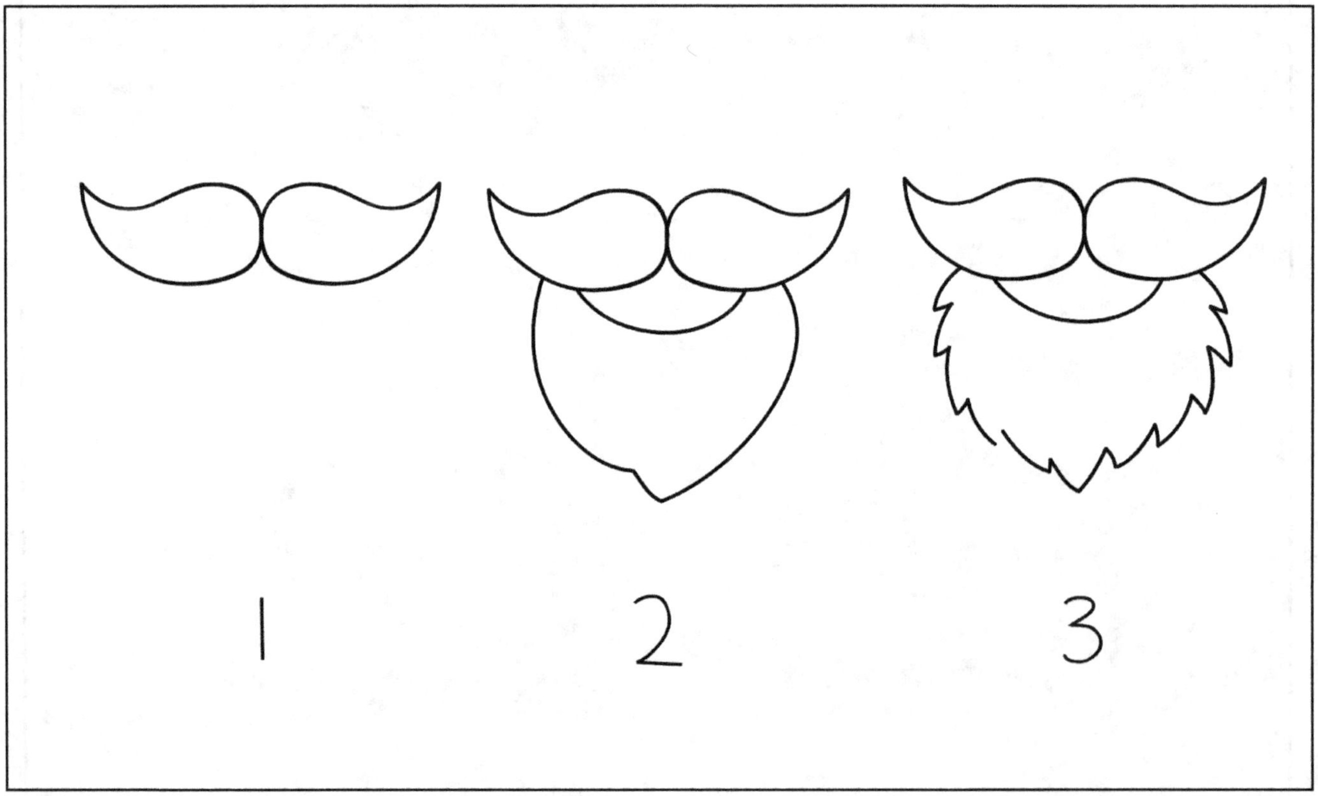

1   2   3

your turn to draw

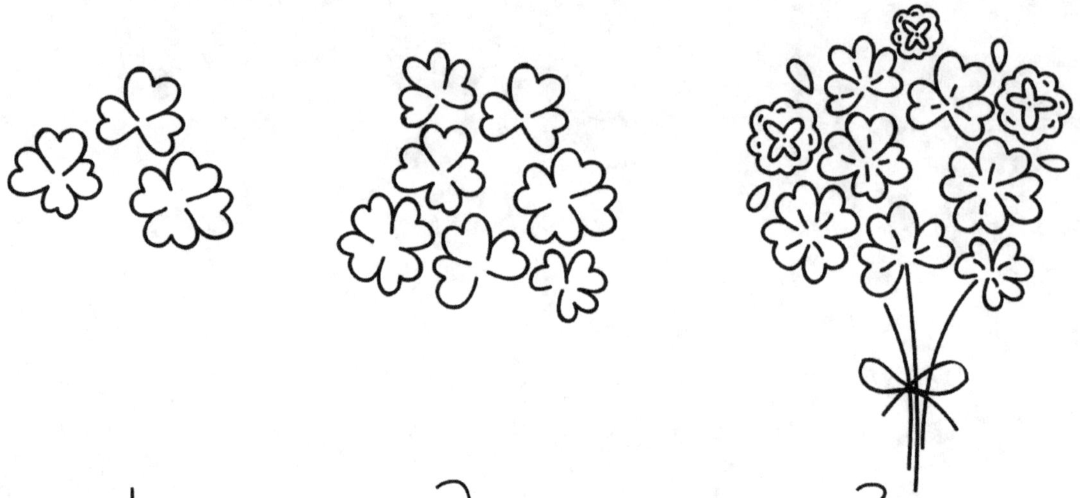

1   2   3

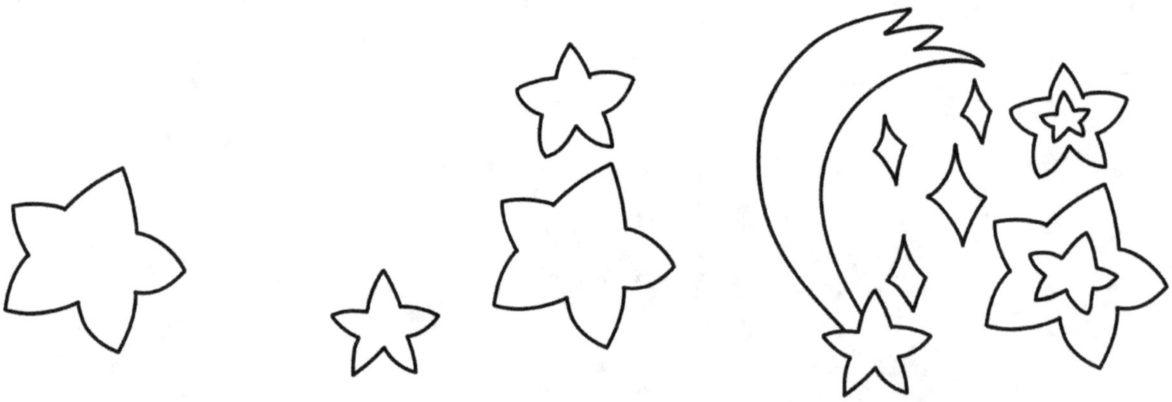

1   2   3

your turn to draw

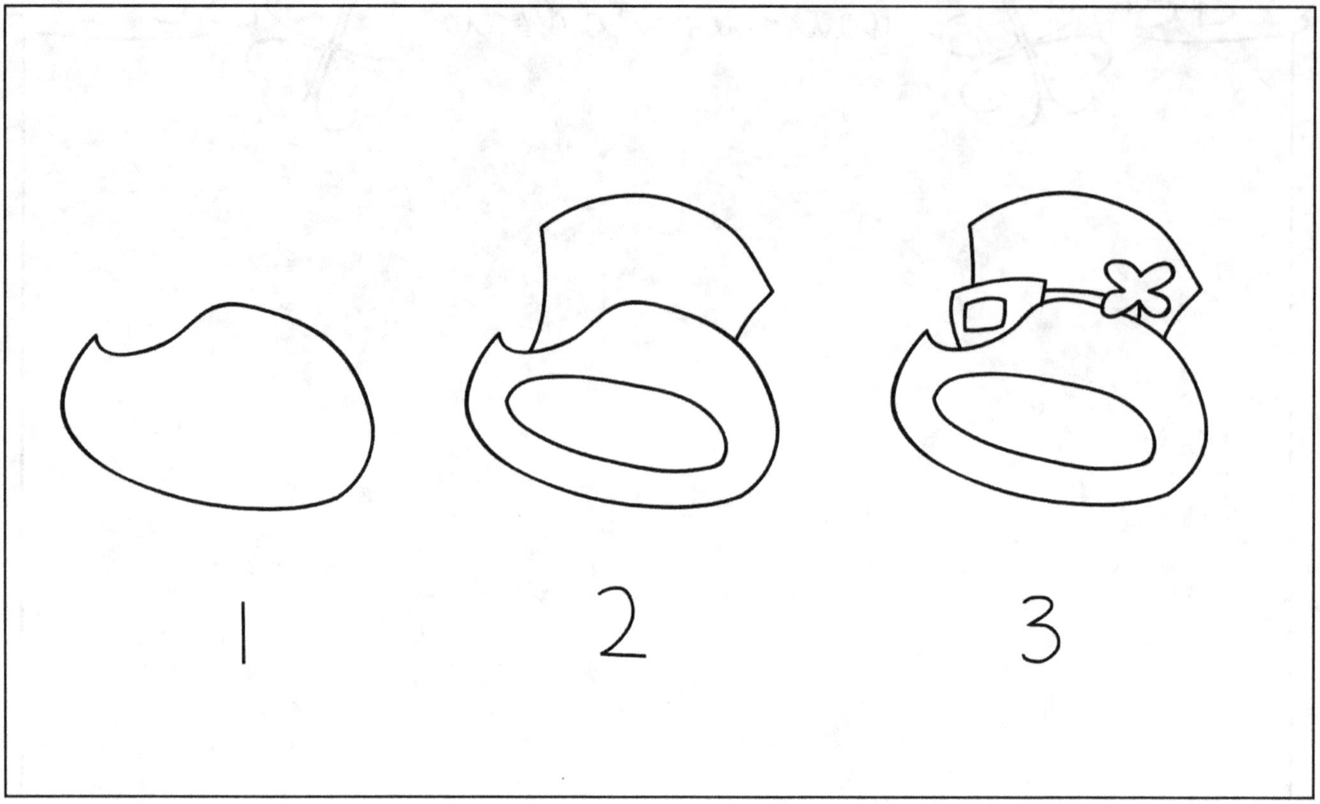

1   2   3

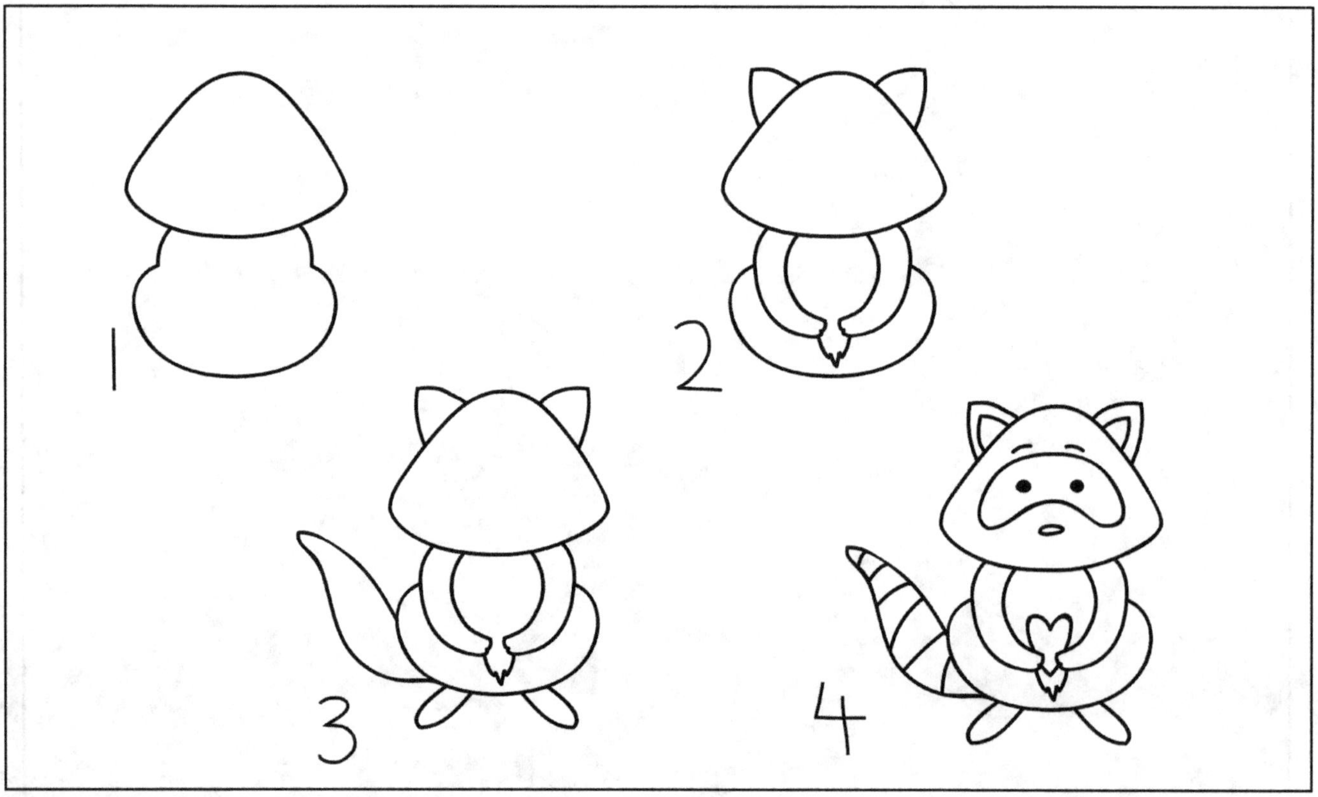

1   2

3   4

your turn to draw

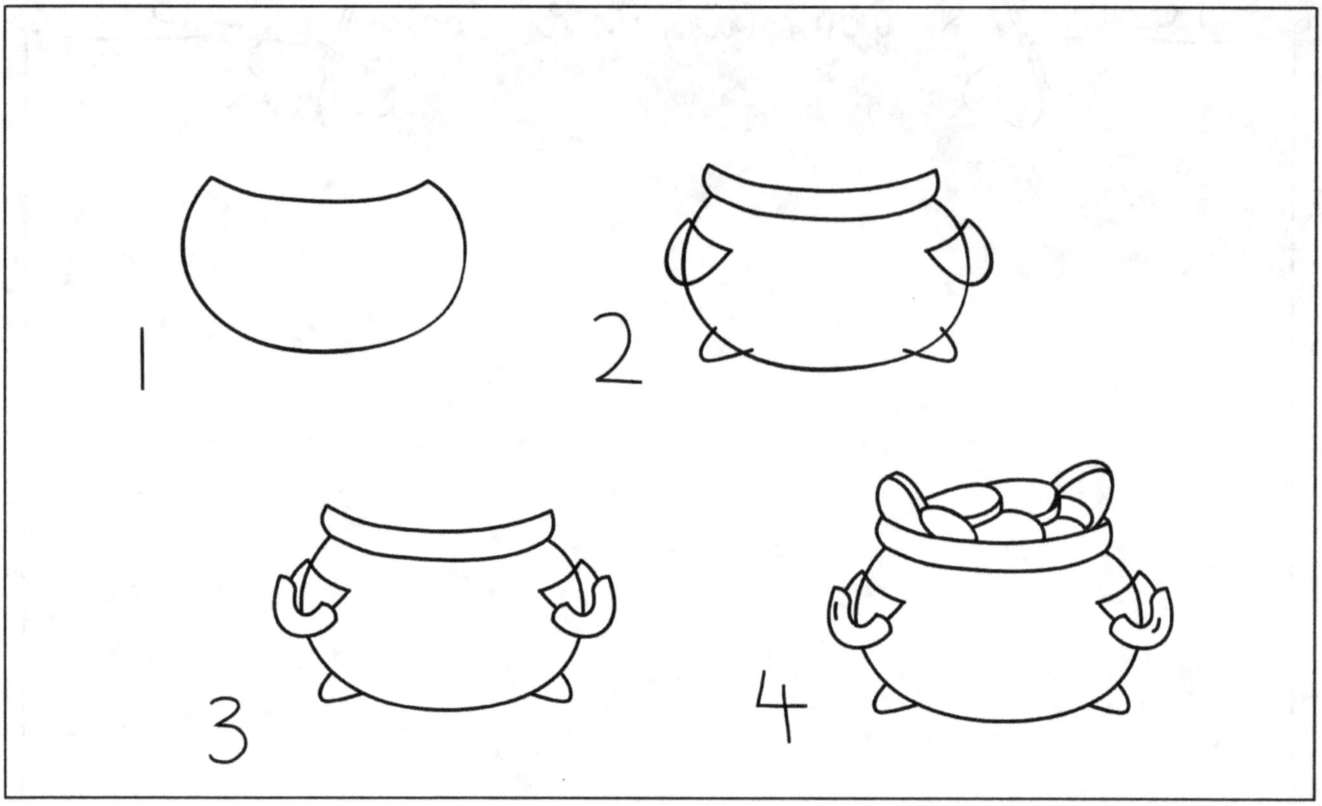

1

2

3

4

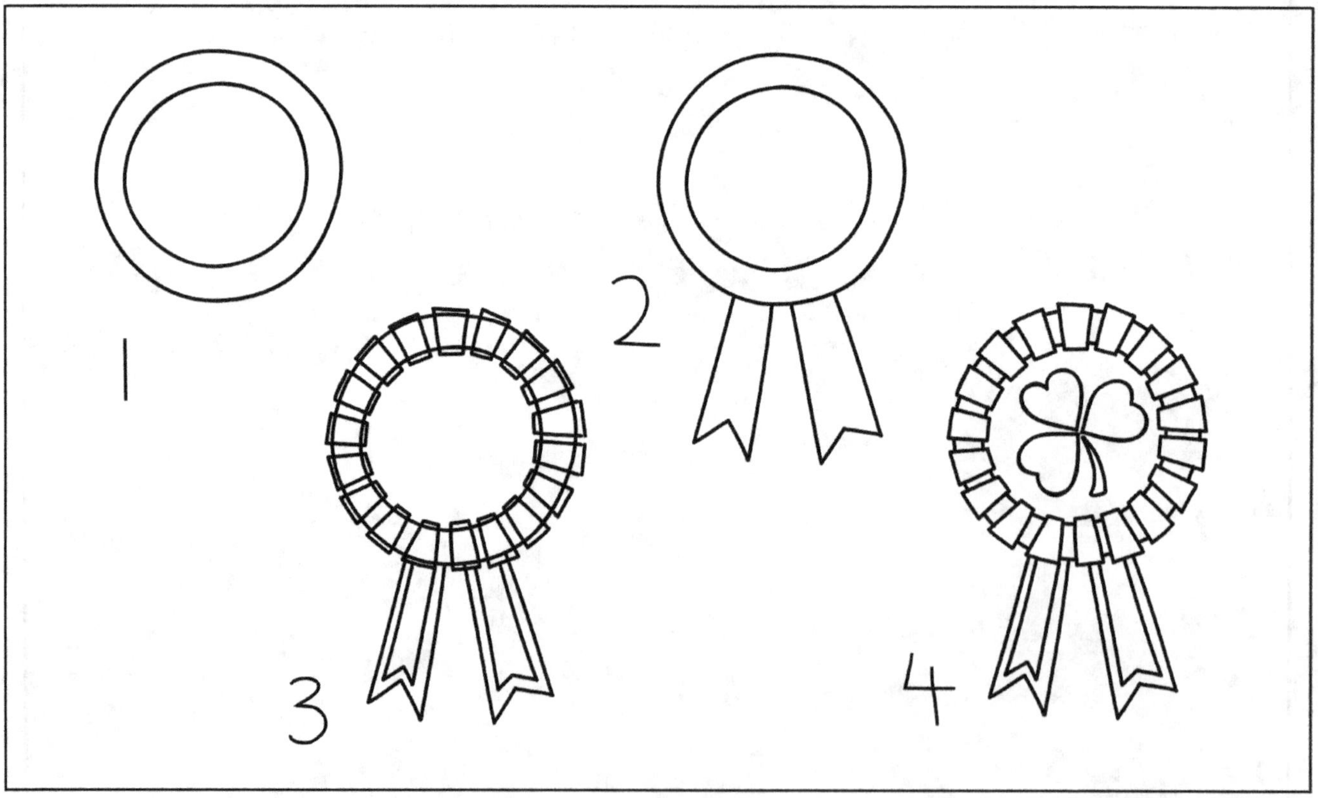

1

2

3

4

your turn to draw

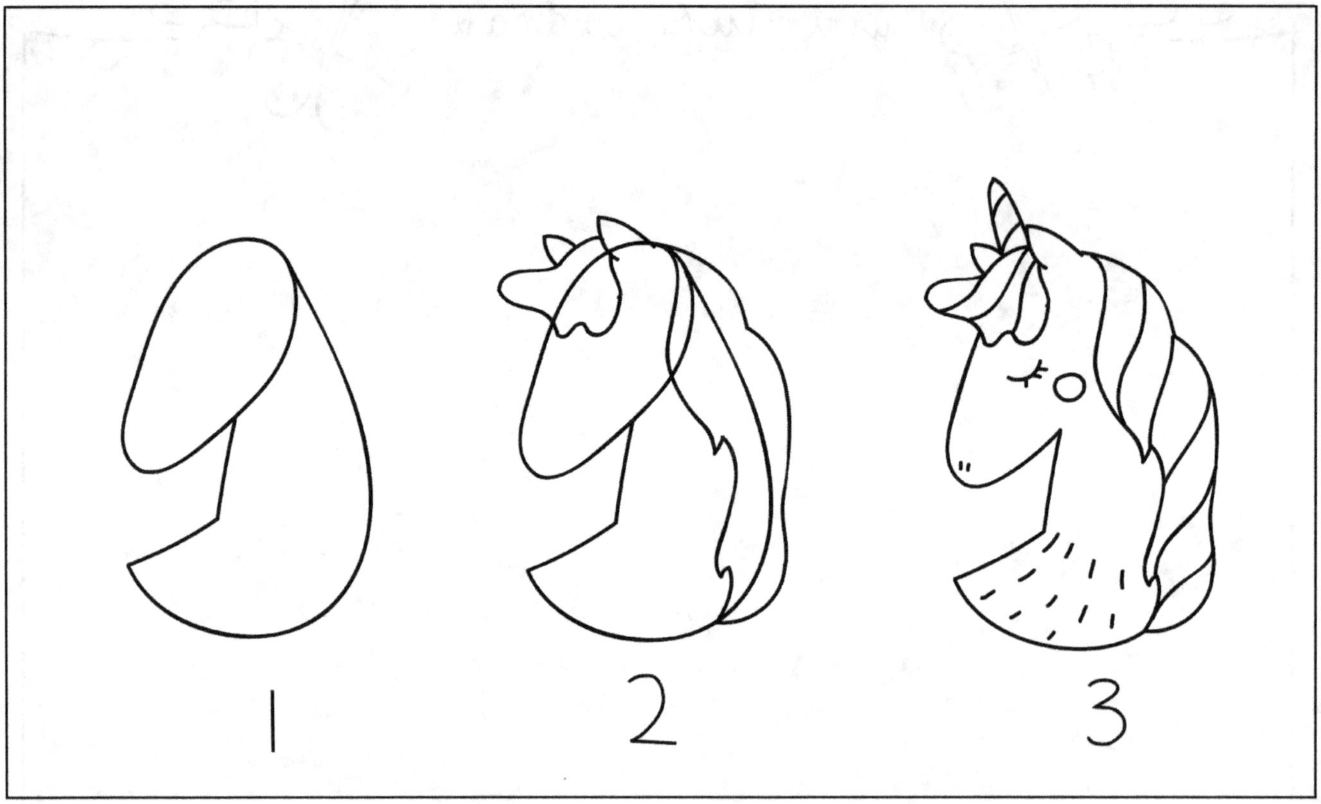

1

2

3

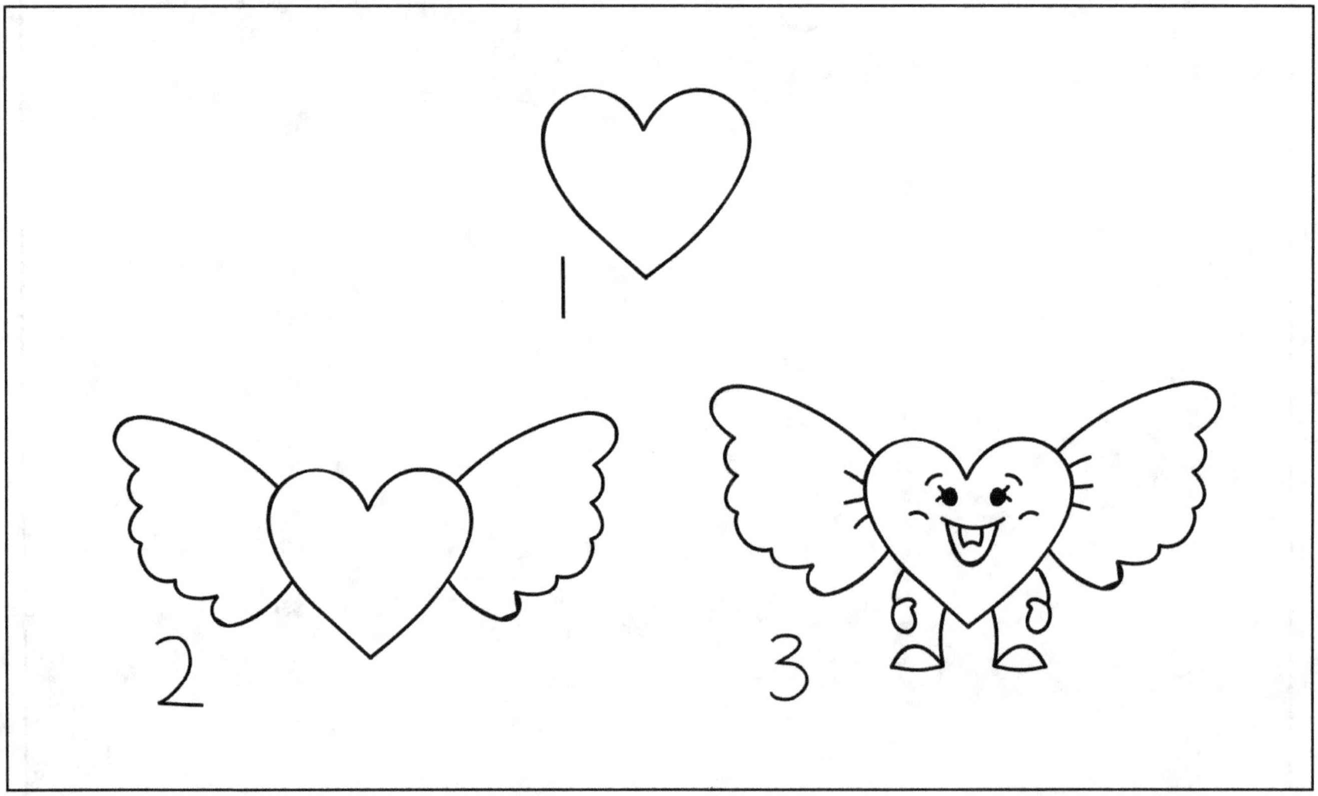

1

2

3

your turn to draw

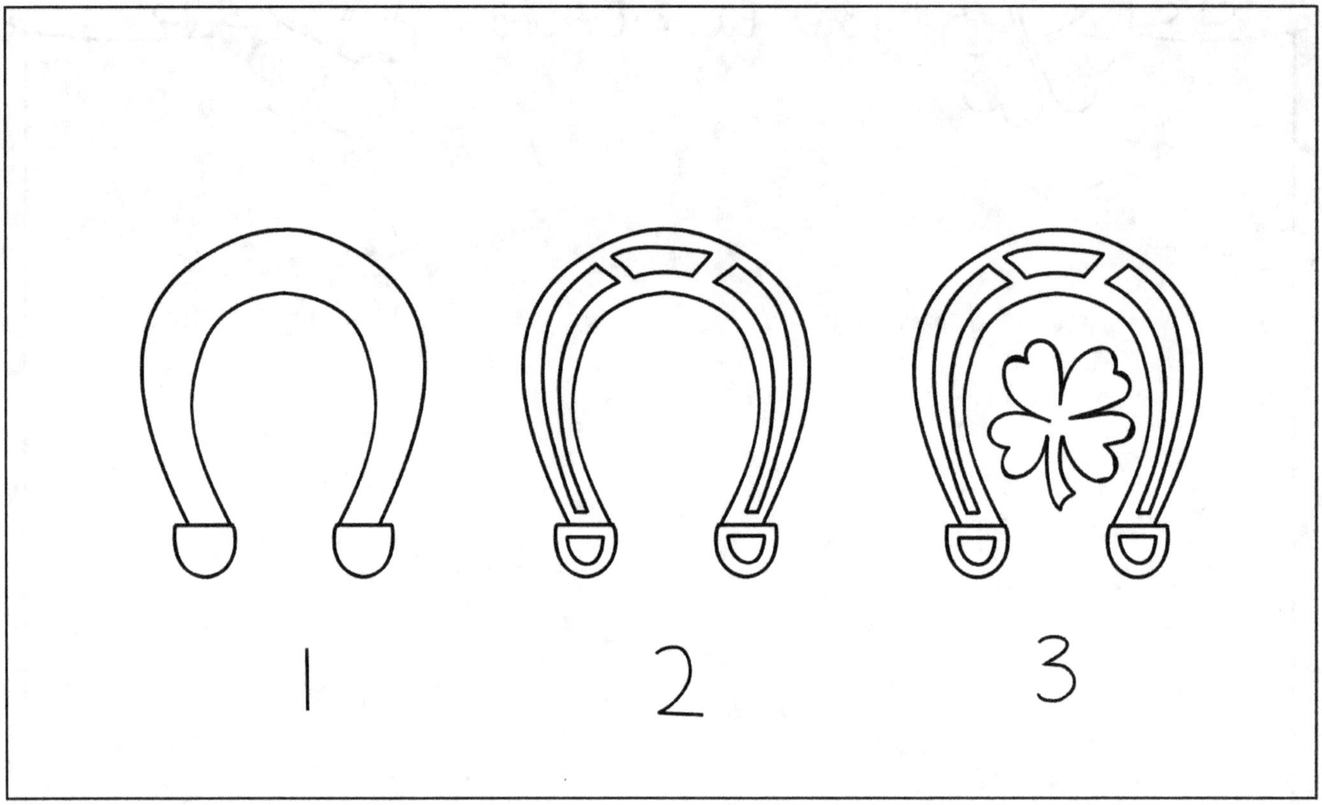

1   2   3

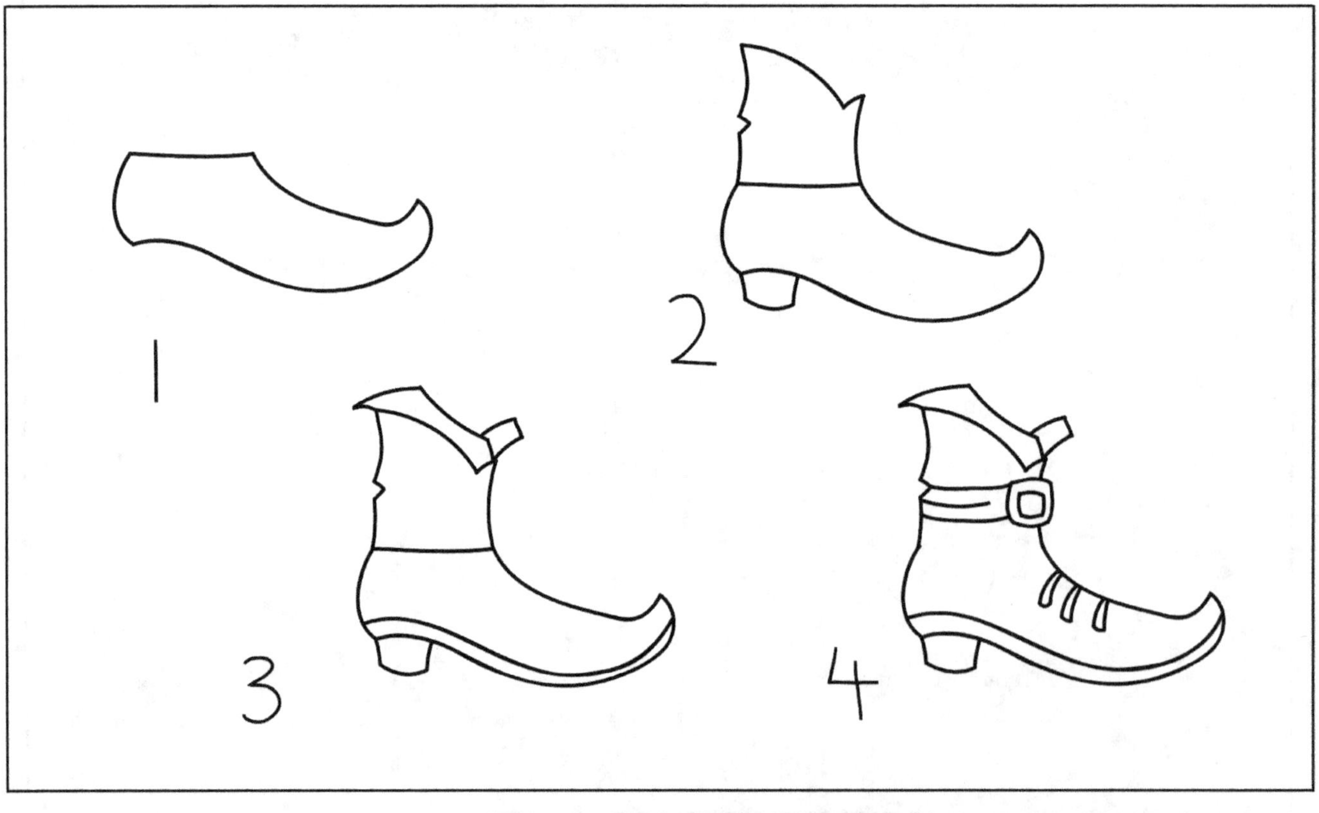

1   2

3   4

your turn to draw

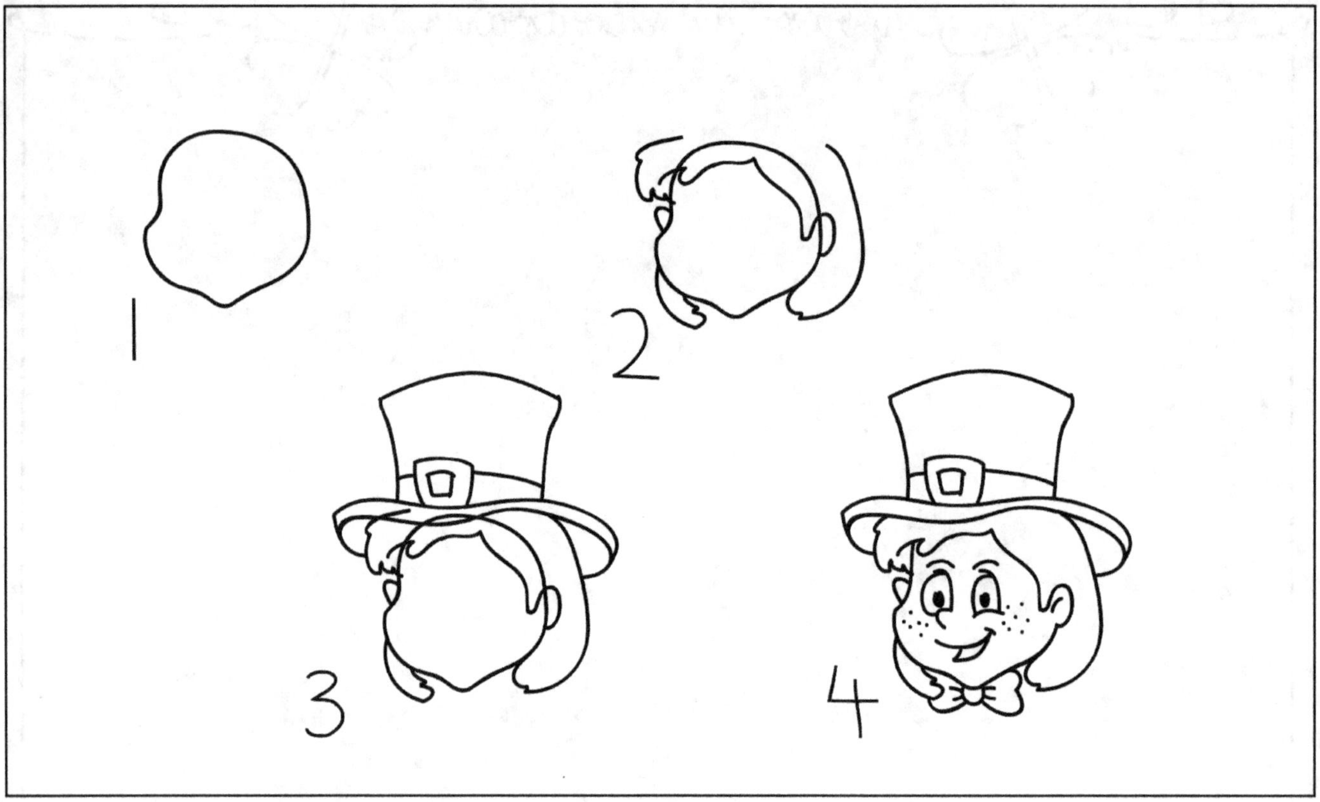

1

2

3

4

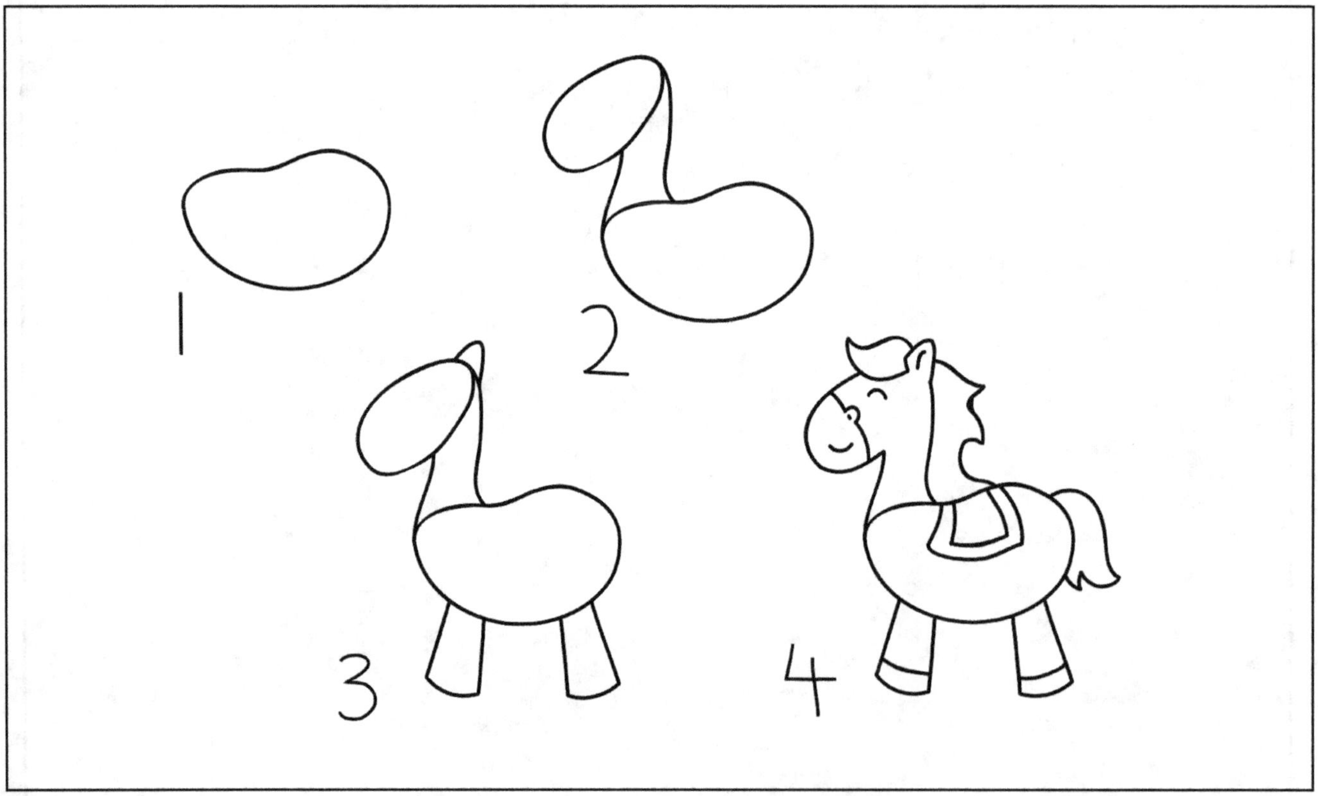

1

2

3

4

your turn to draw

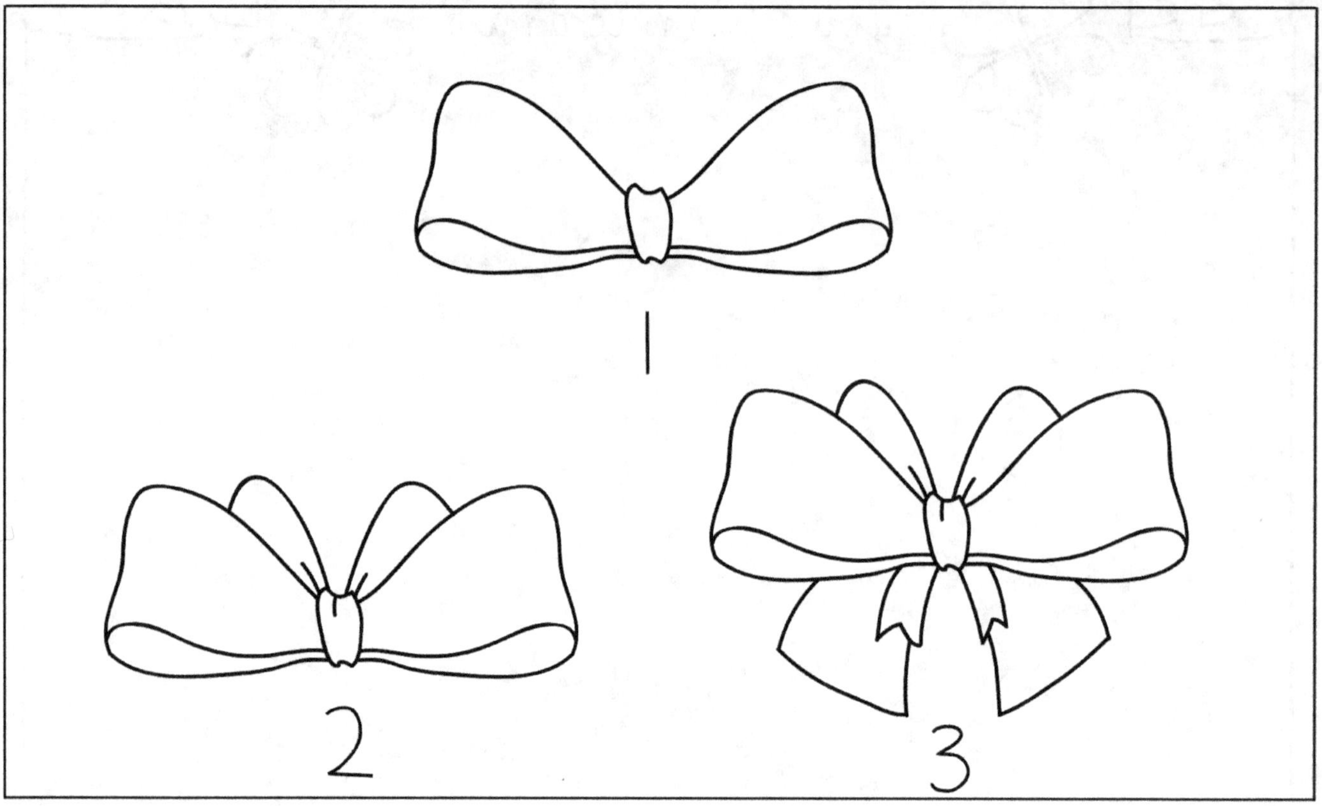

1

2

3

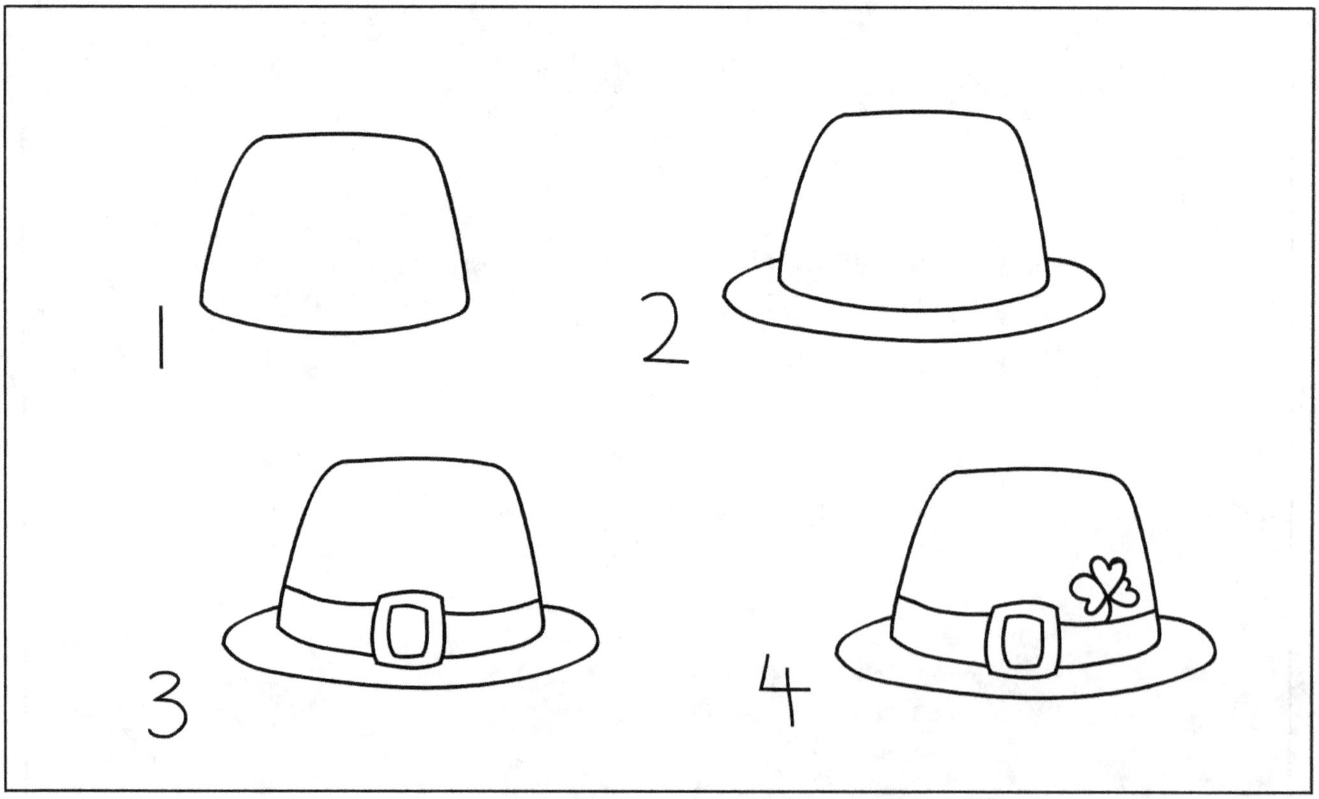

1

2

3

4

your turn to draw

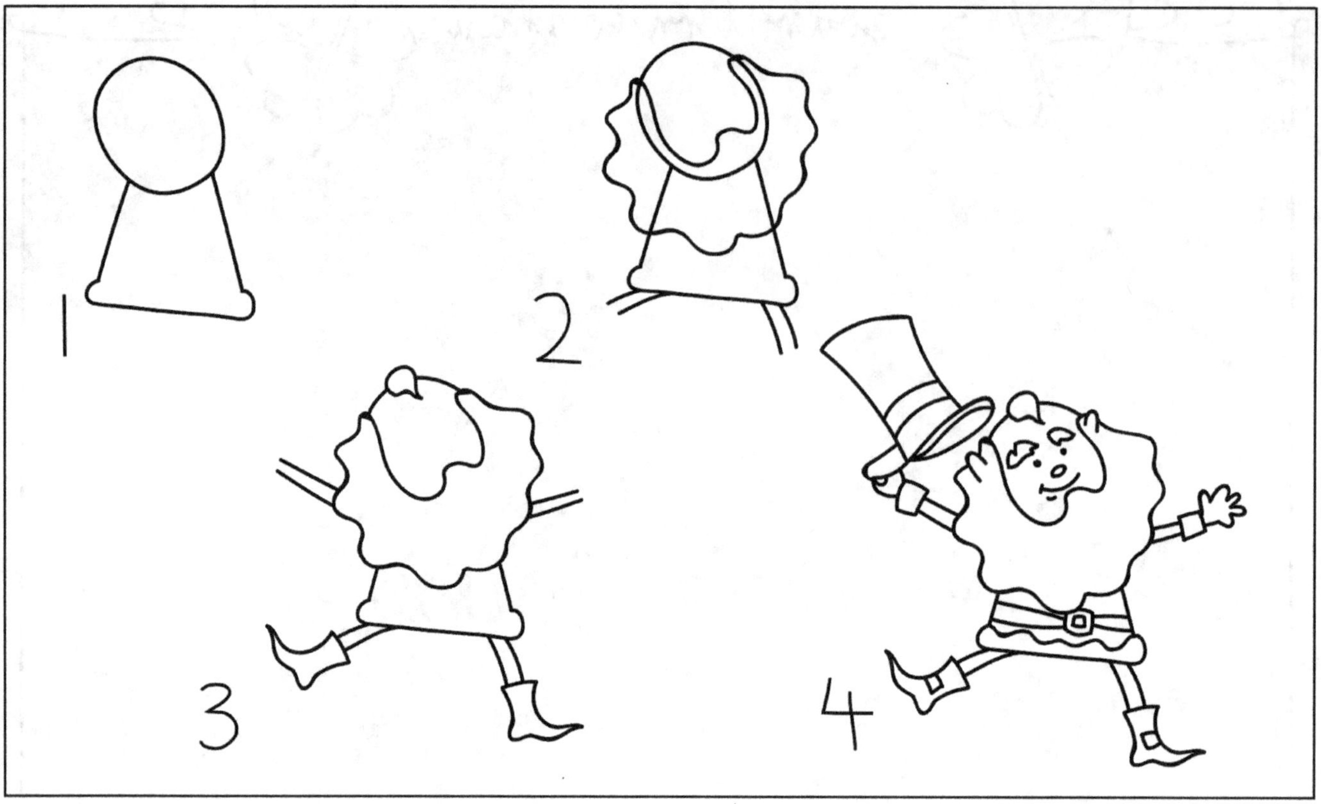

1

2

3

4

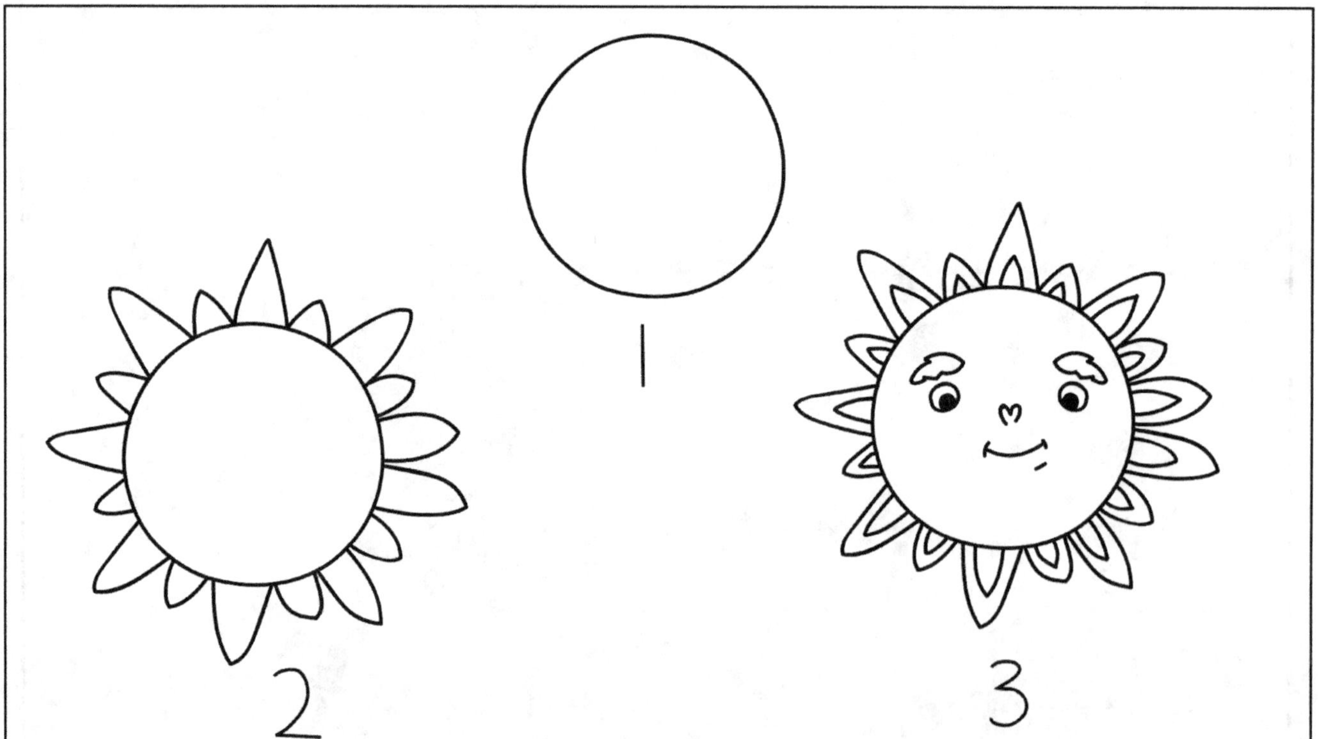

1

2

3

your turn to draw

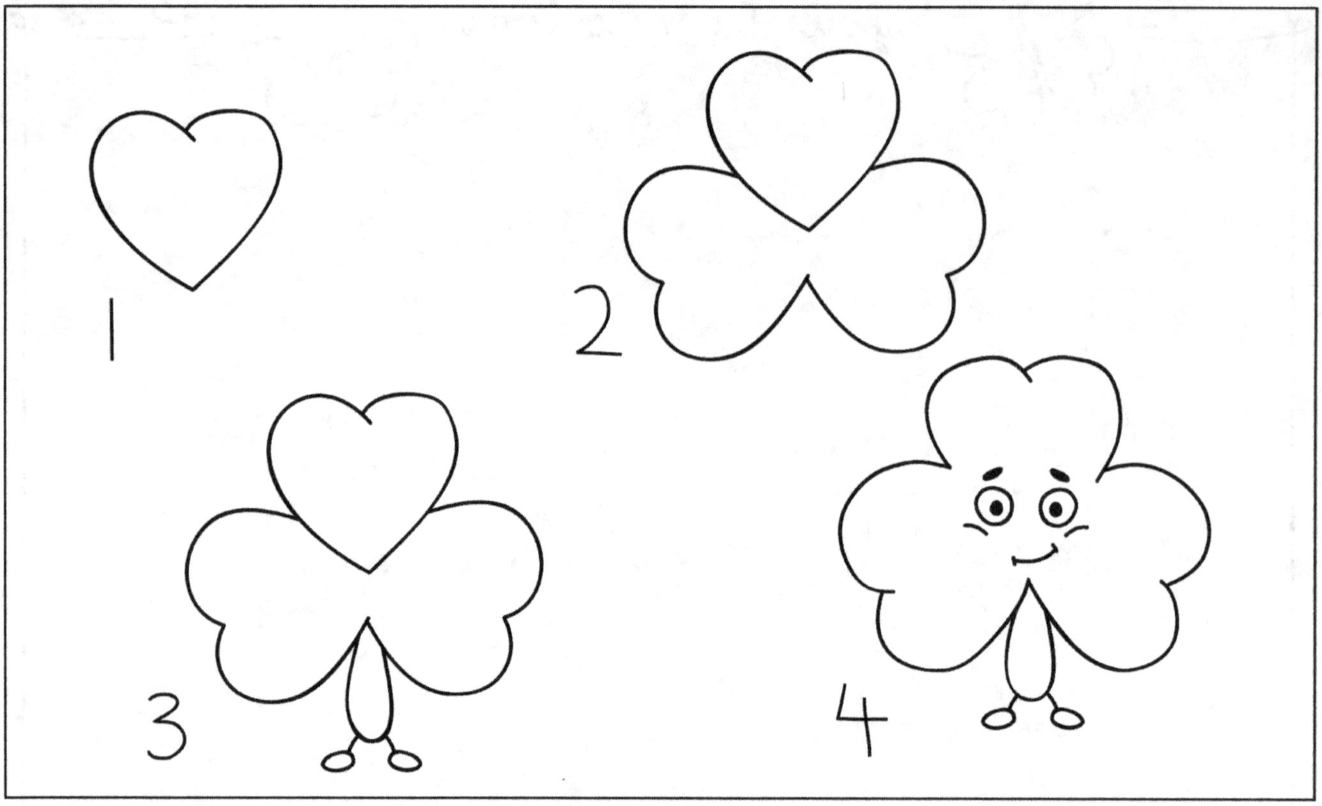

1

2

3

4

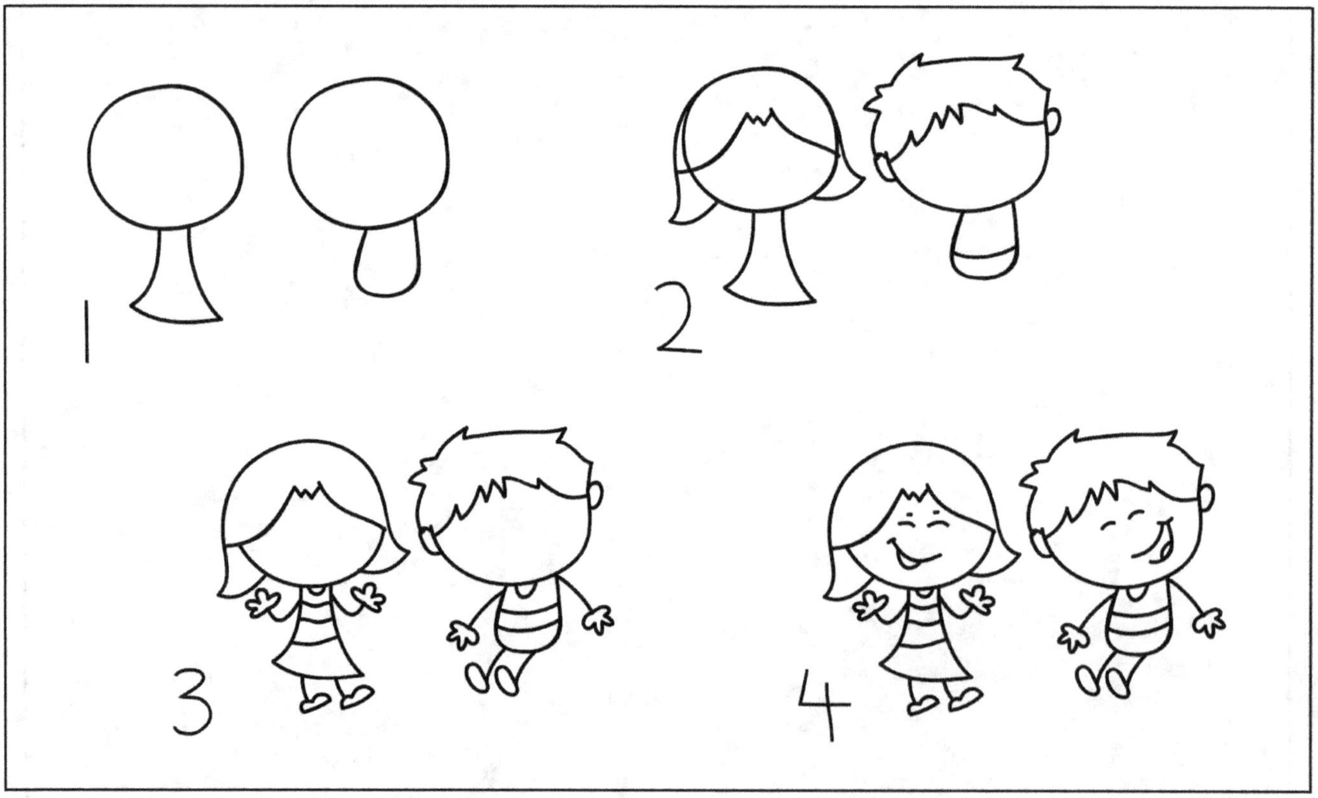

1

2

3

4

your turn to draw

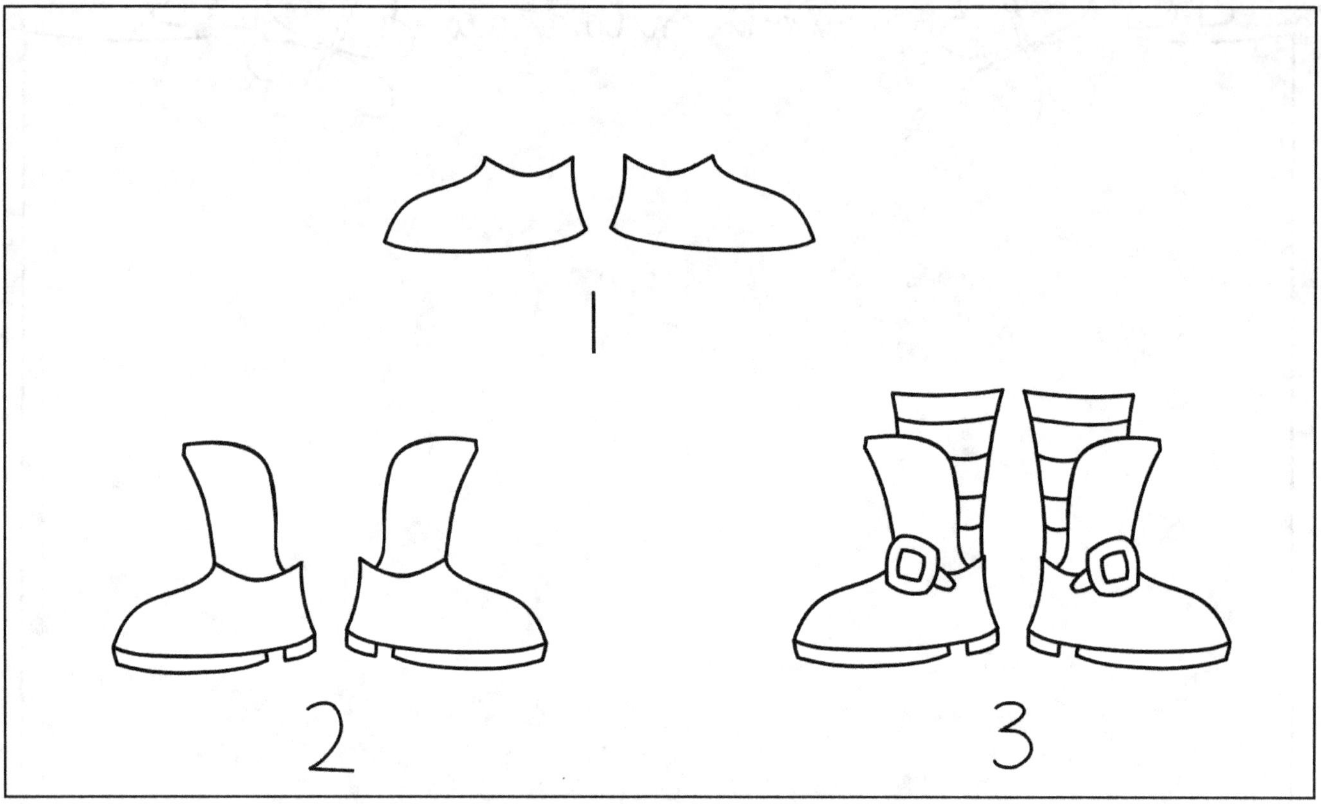

2

3

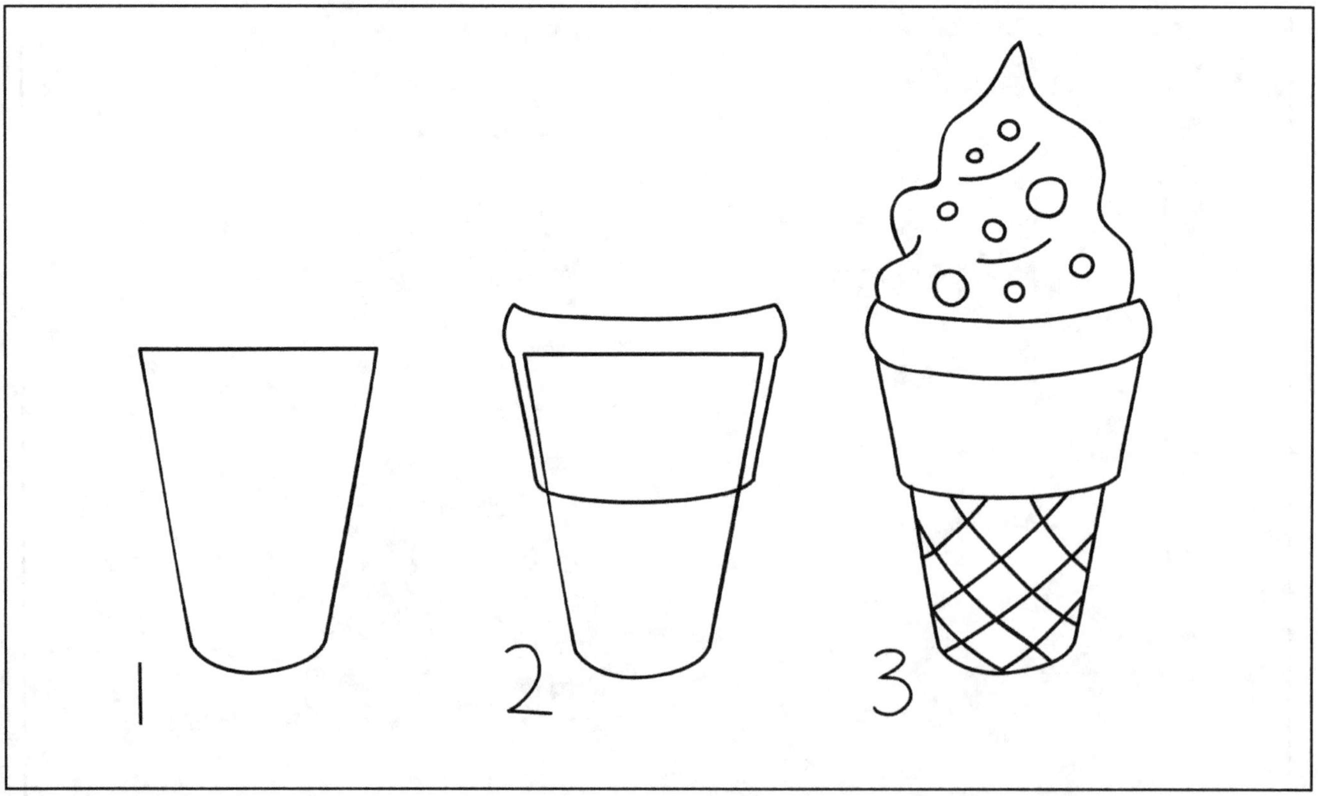

1

2

3

your turn to draw

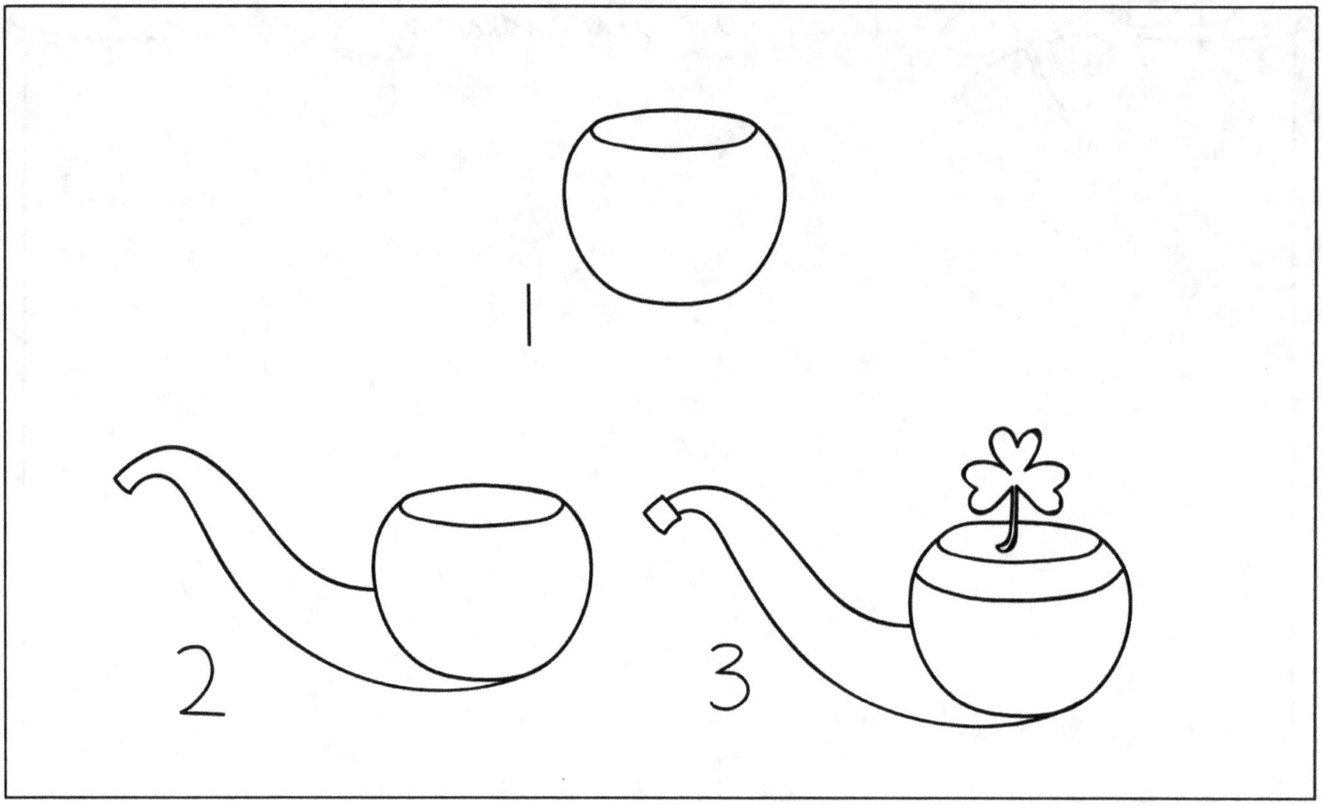

1

2

3

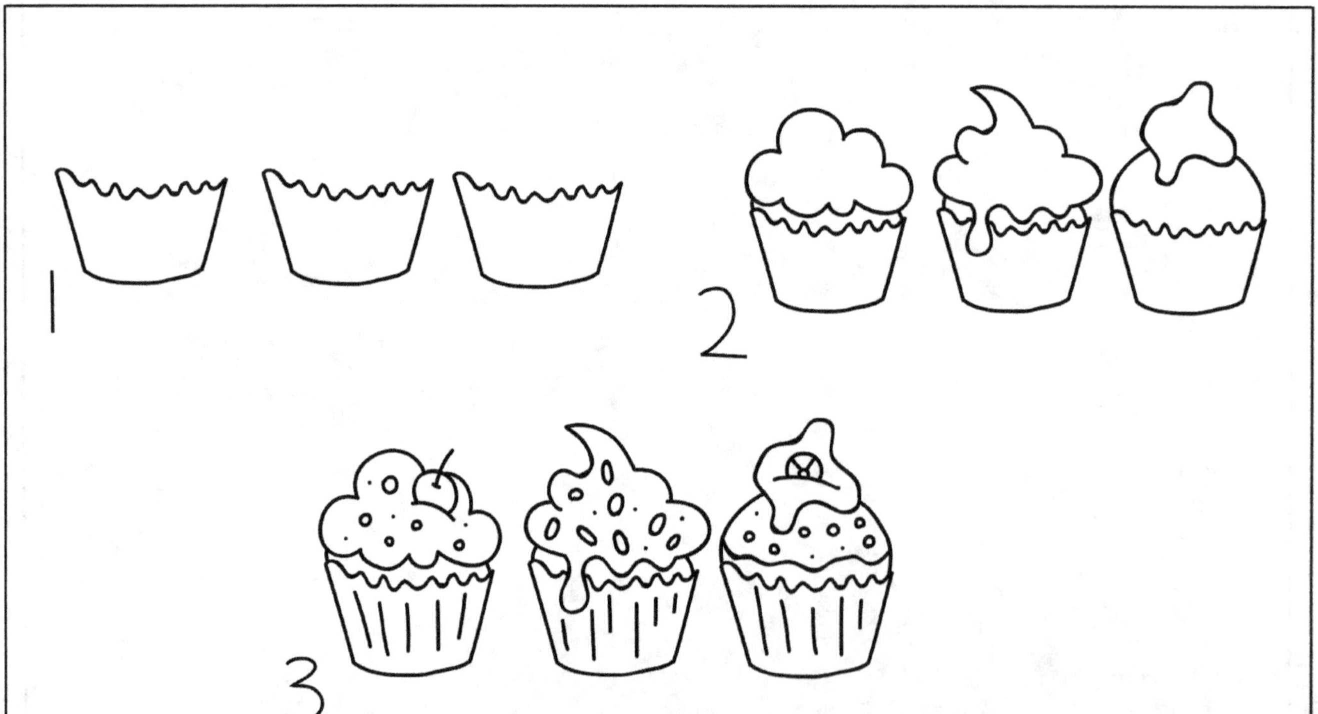

1

2

3

your turn to draw

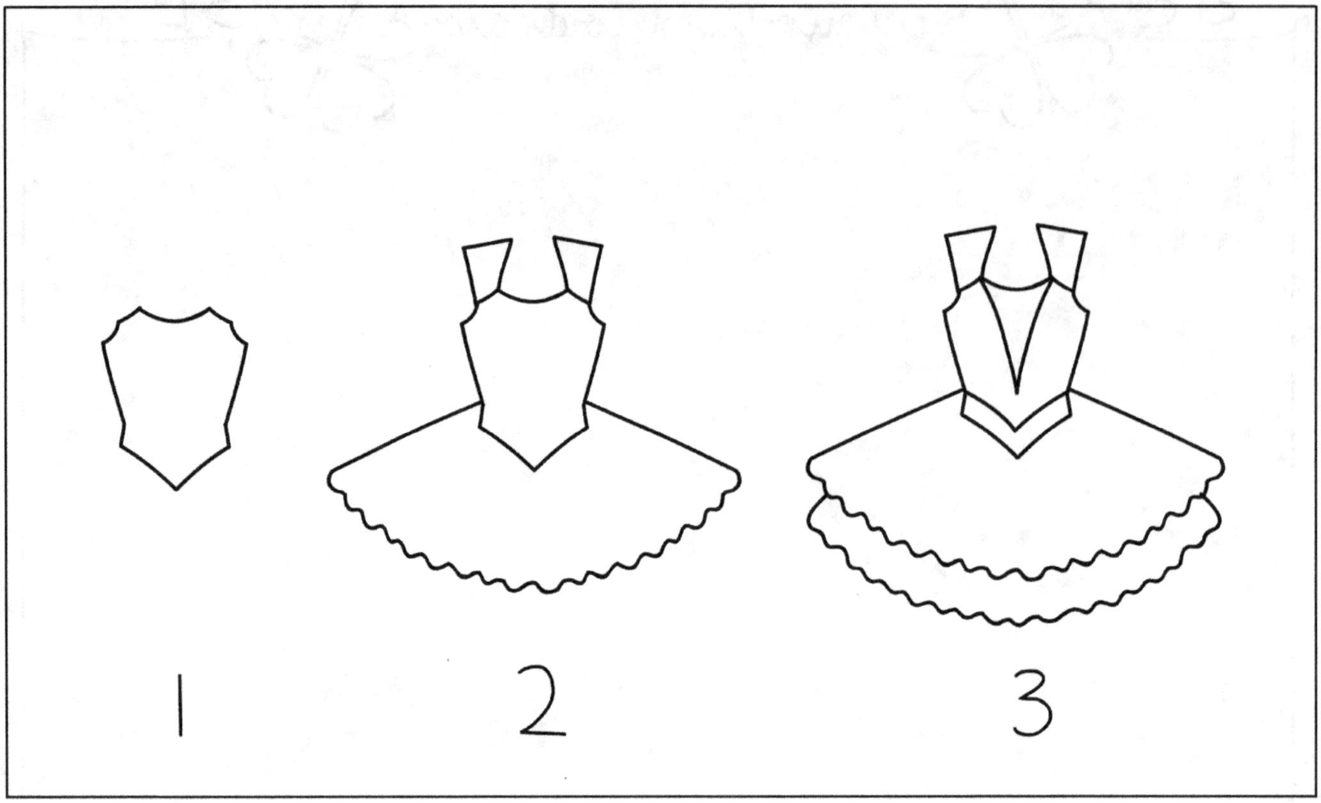

1

2

3

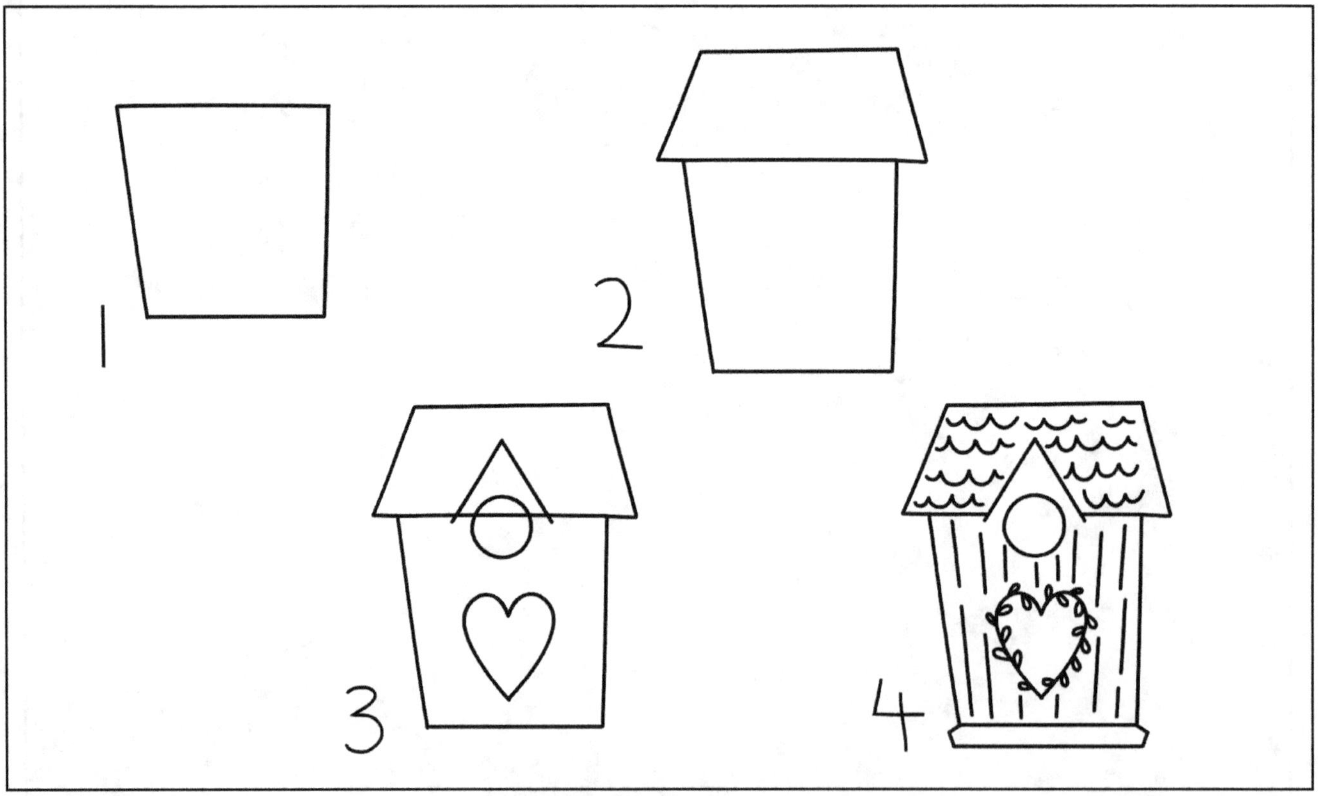

1

2

3

4

your turn to draw

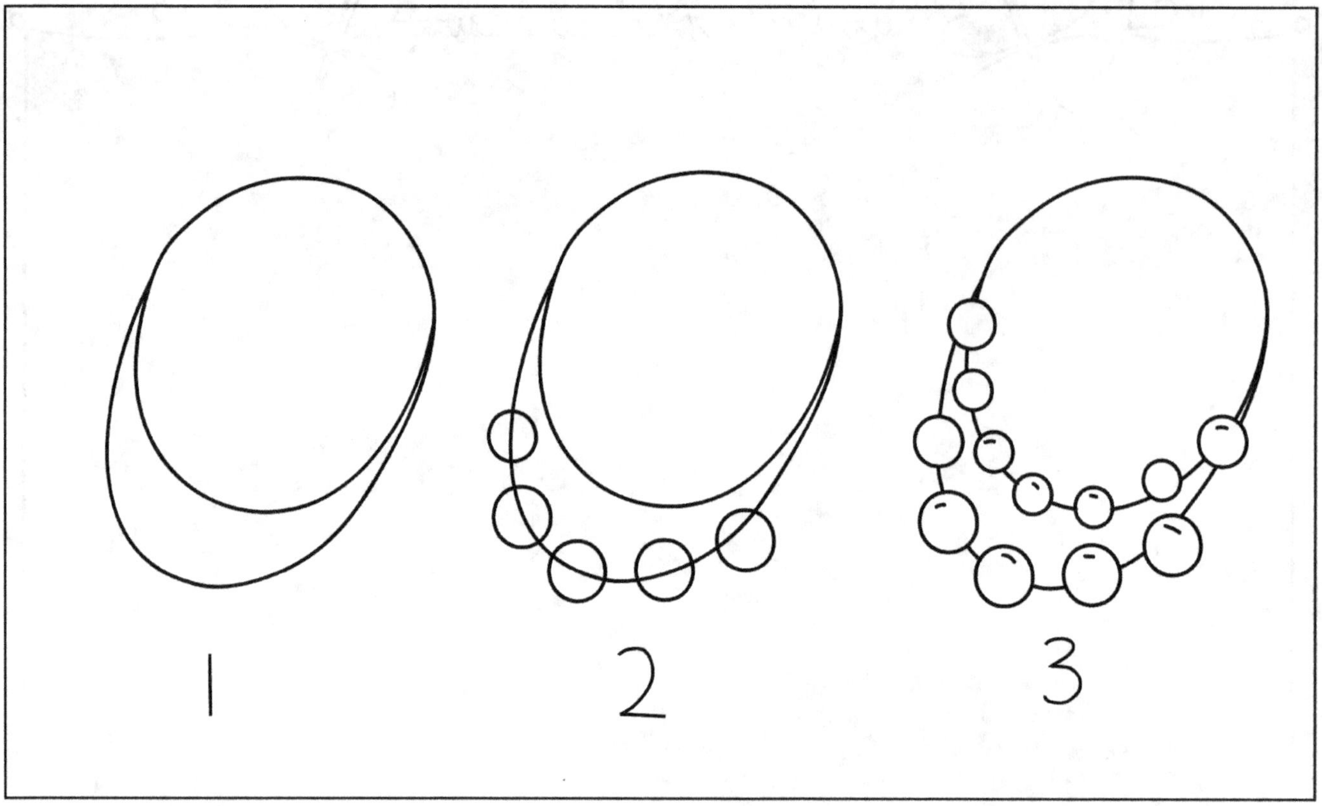

1 2 3

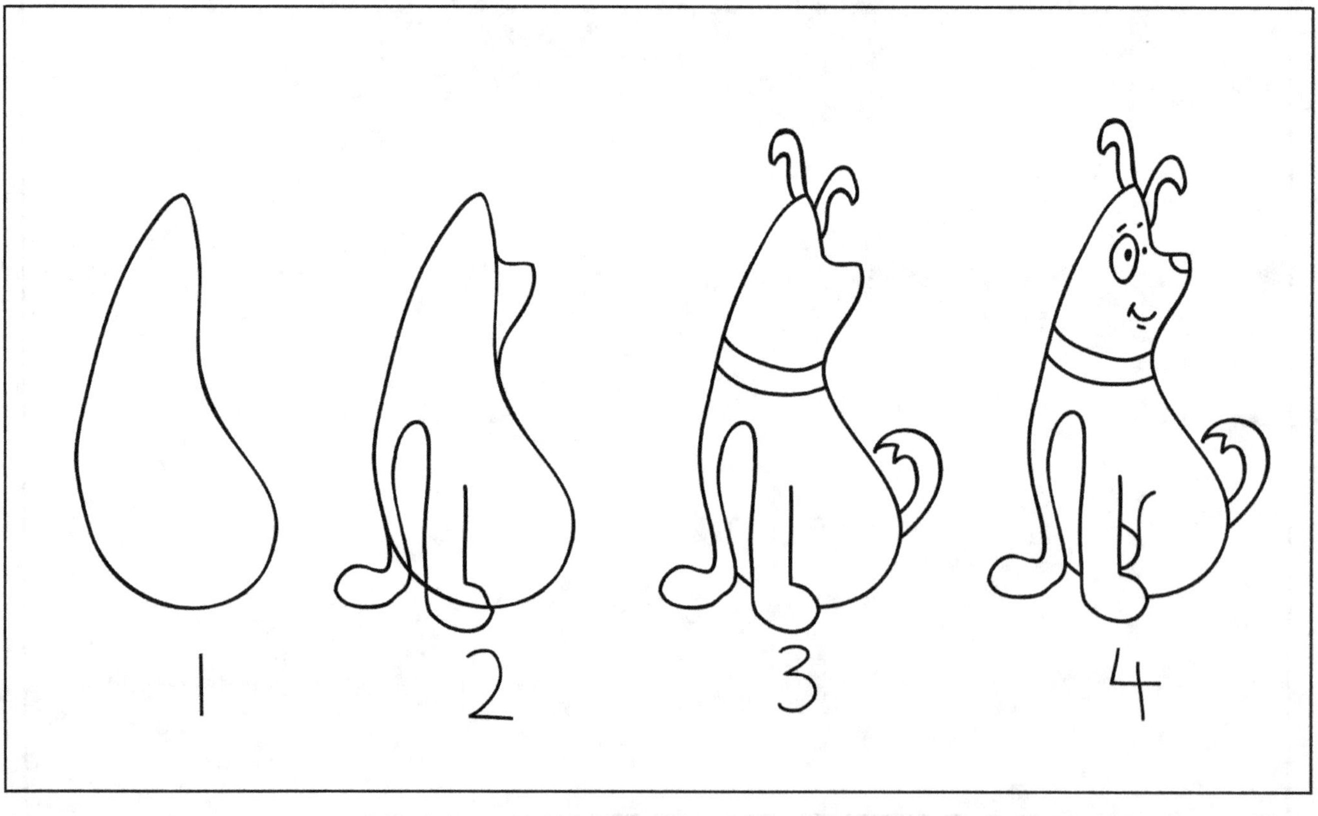

1 2 3 4

your turn to draw

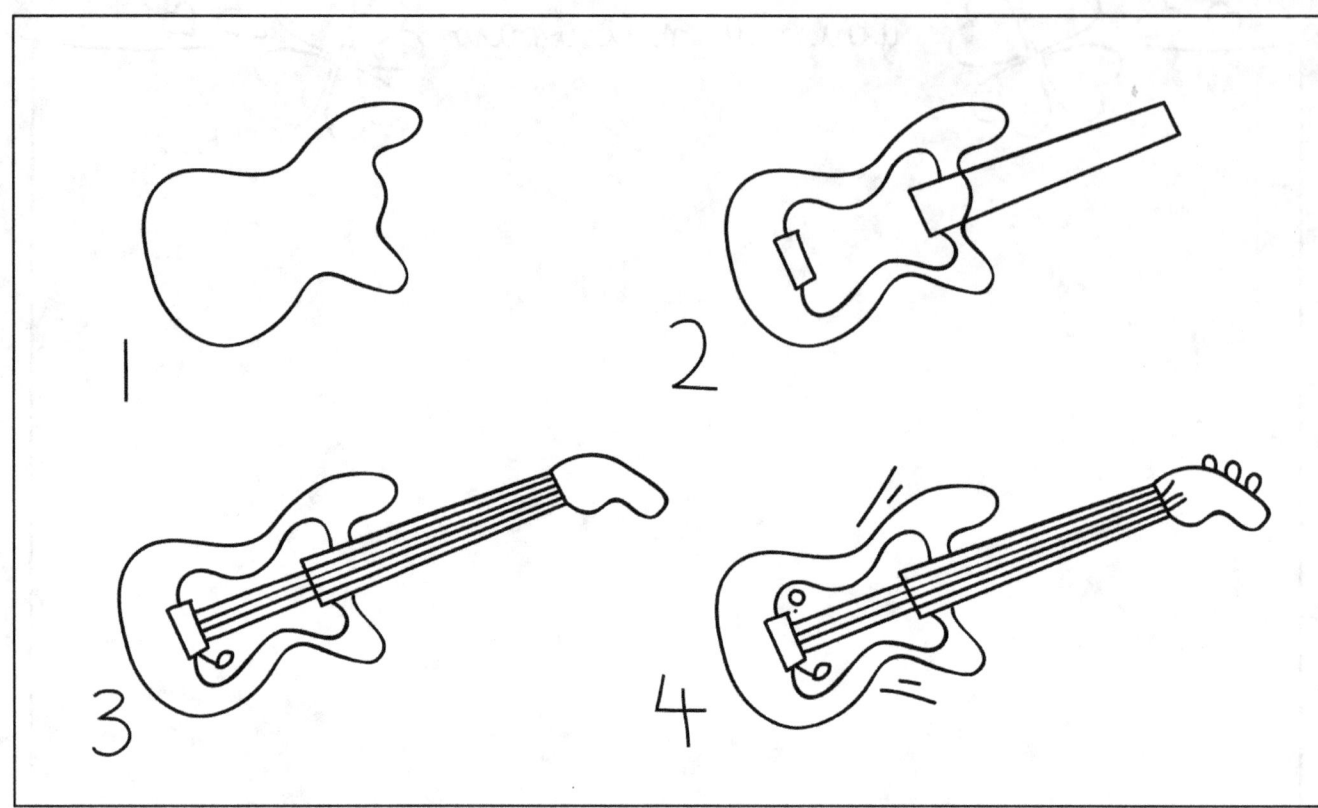

SHAM

|

SHAM
ROCK

2

SHAM
ROCK

3

your turn to draw

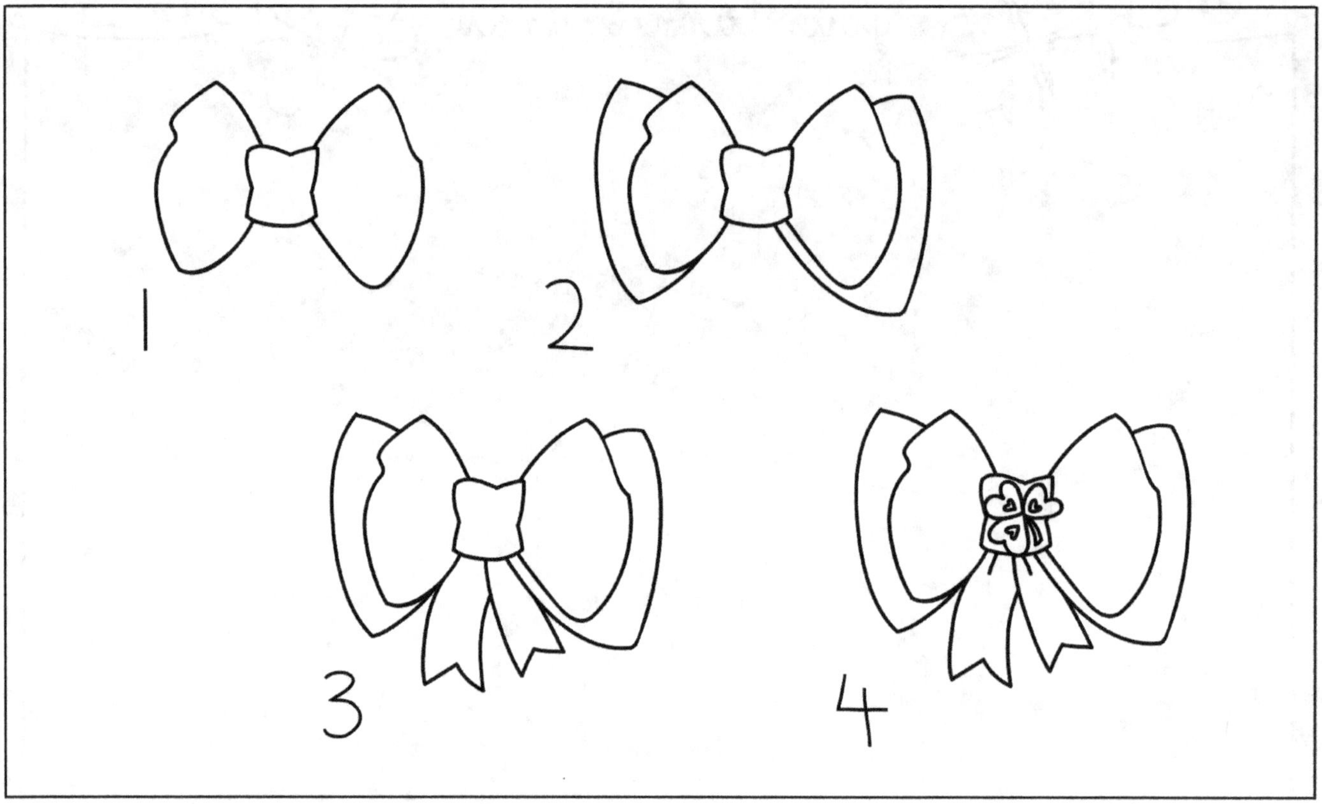

1

2

3

4

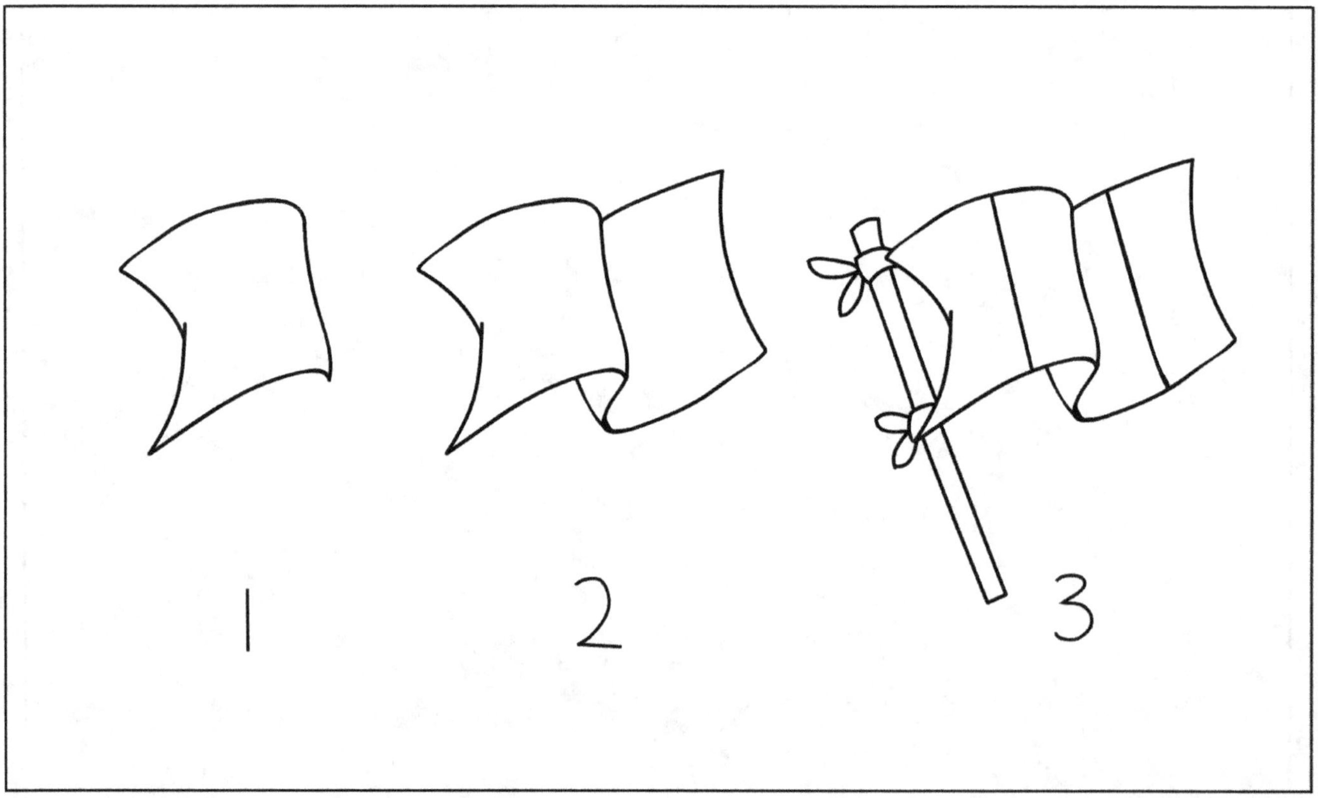

1

2

3

your turn to draw

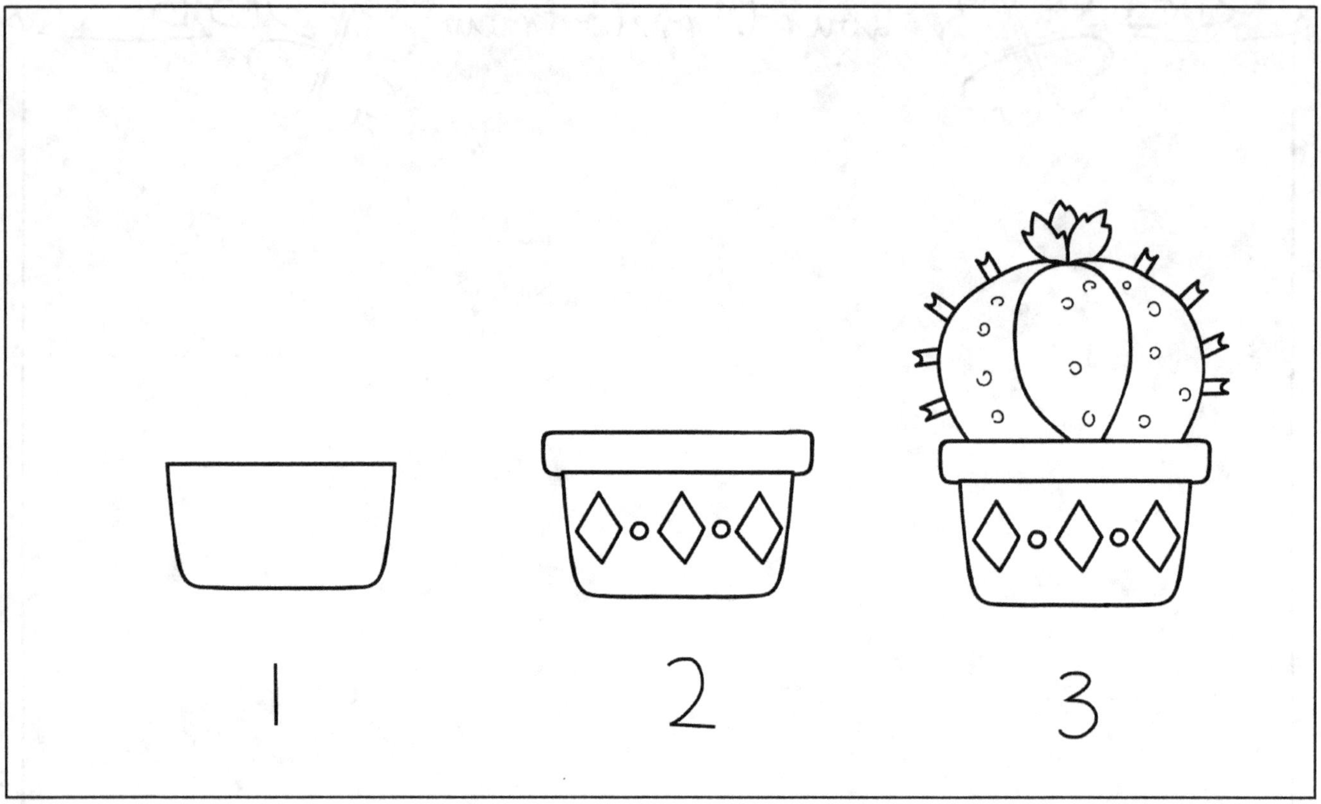

1

2

3

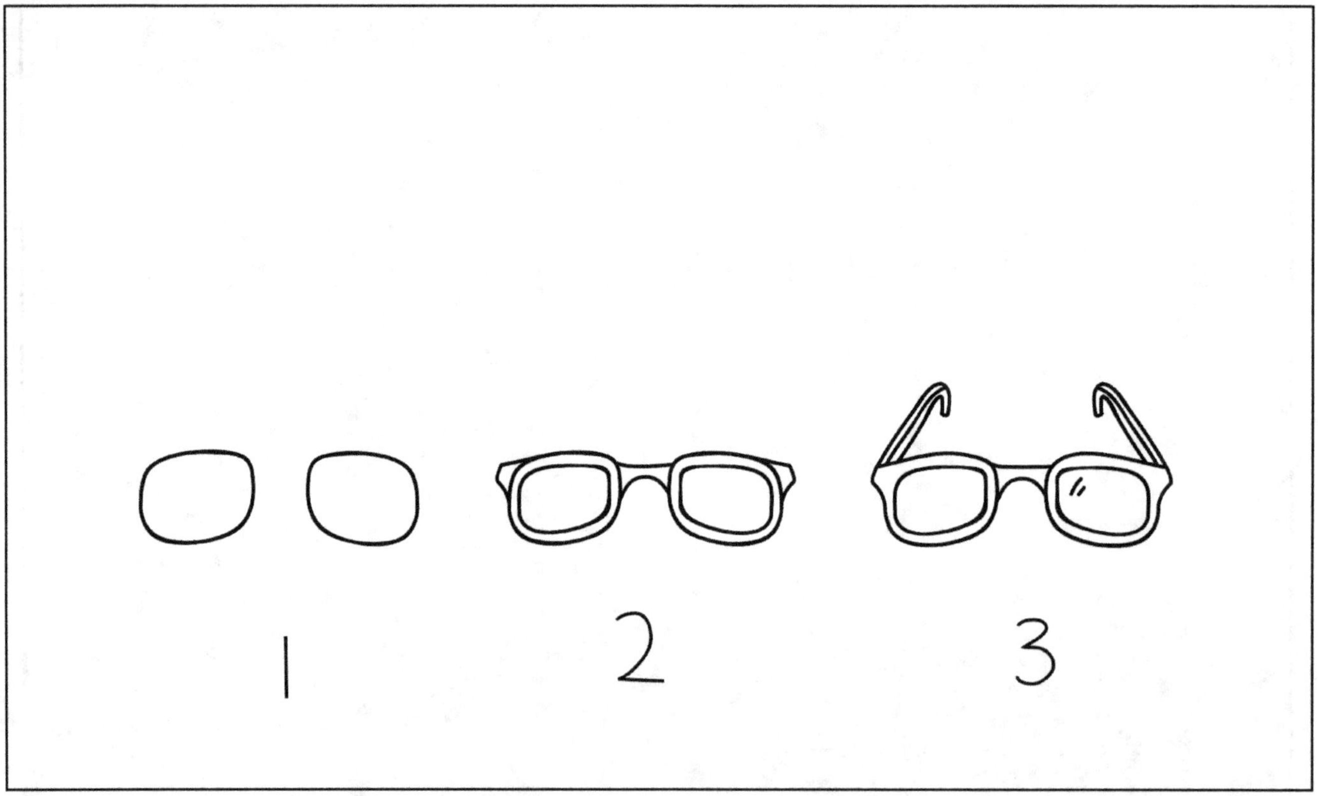

1

2

3

your turn to draw

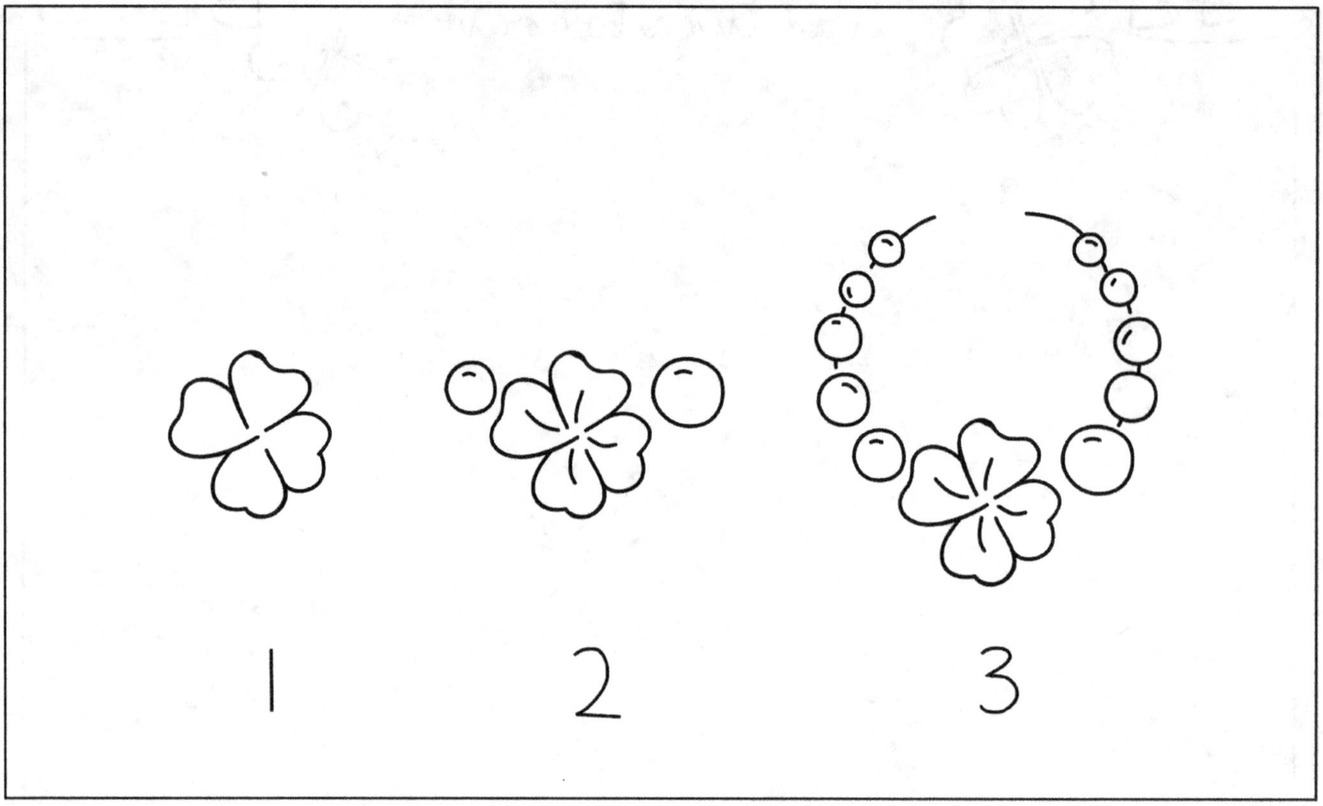

1

2

3

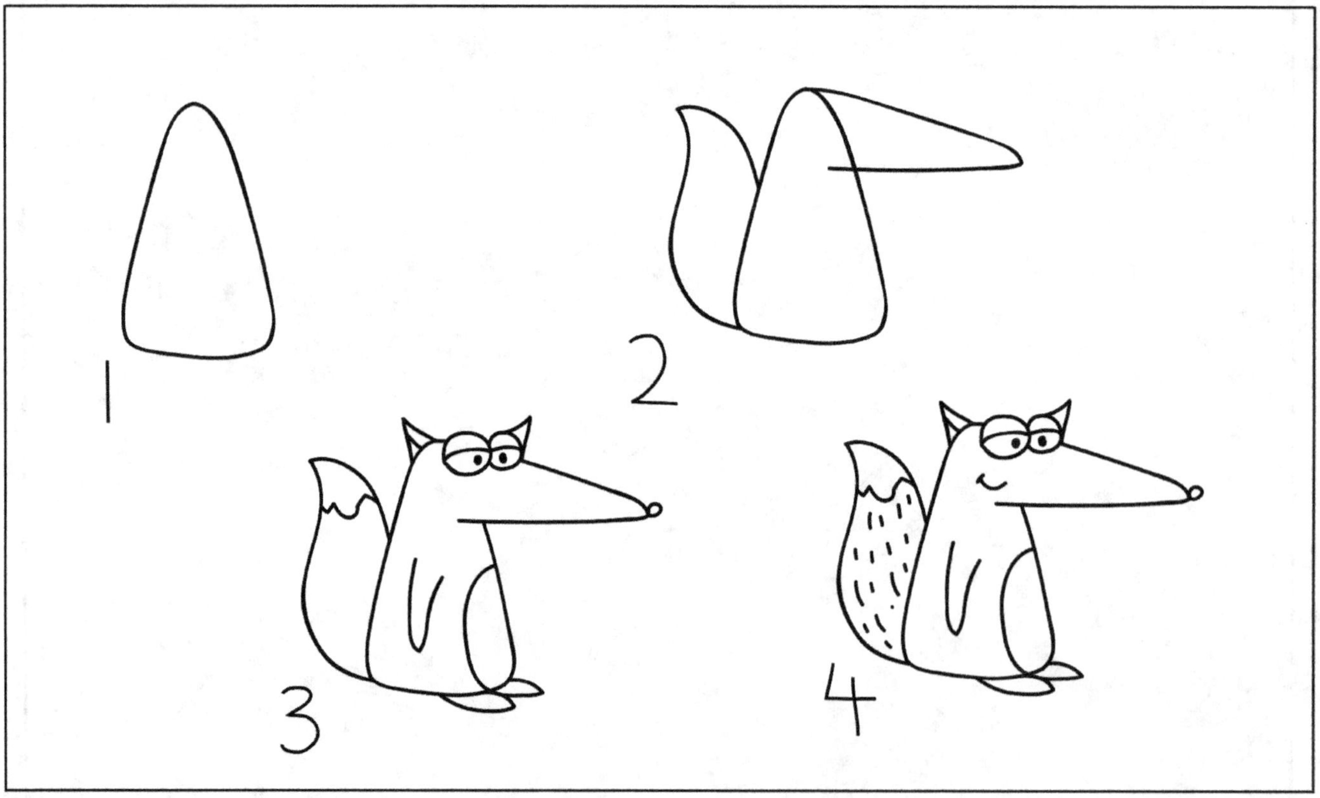

1

2

3

4

your turn to draw

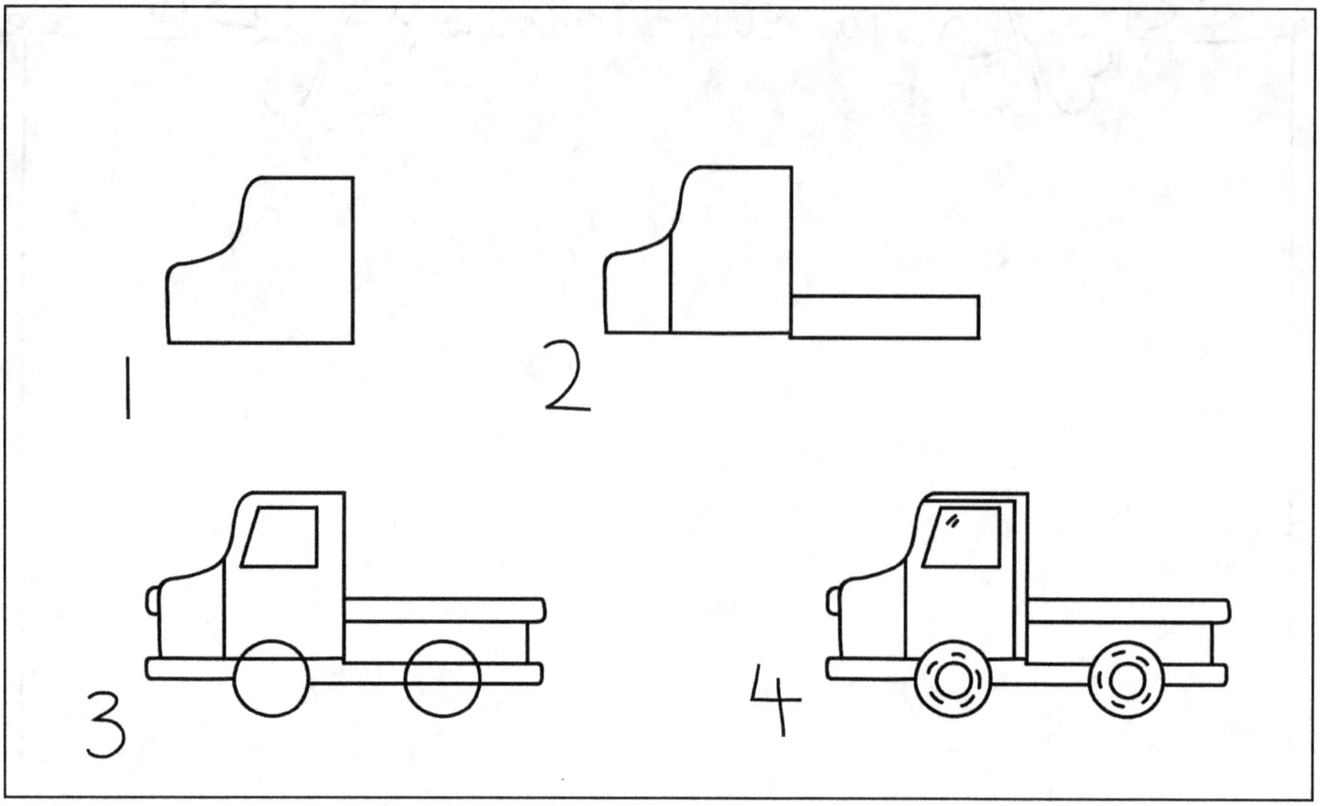

1

2

3

4

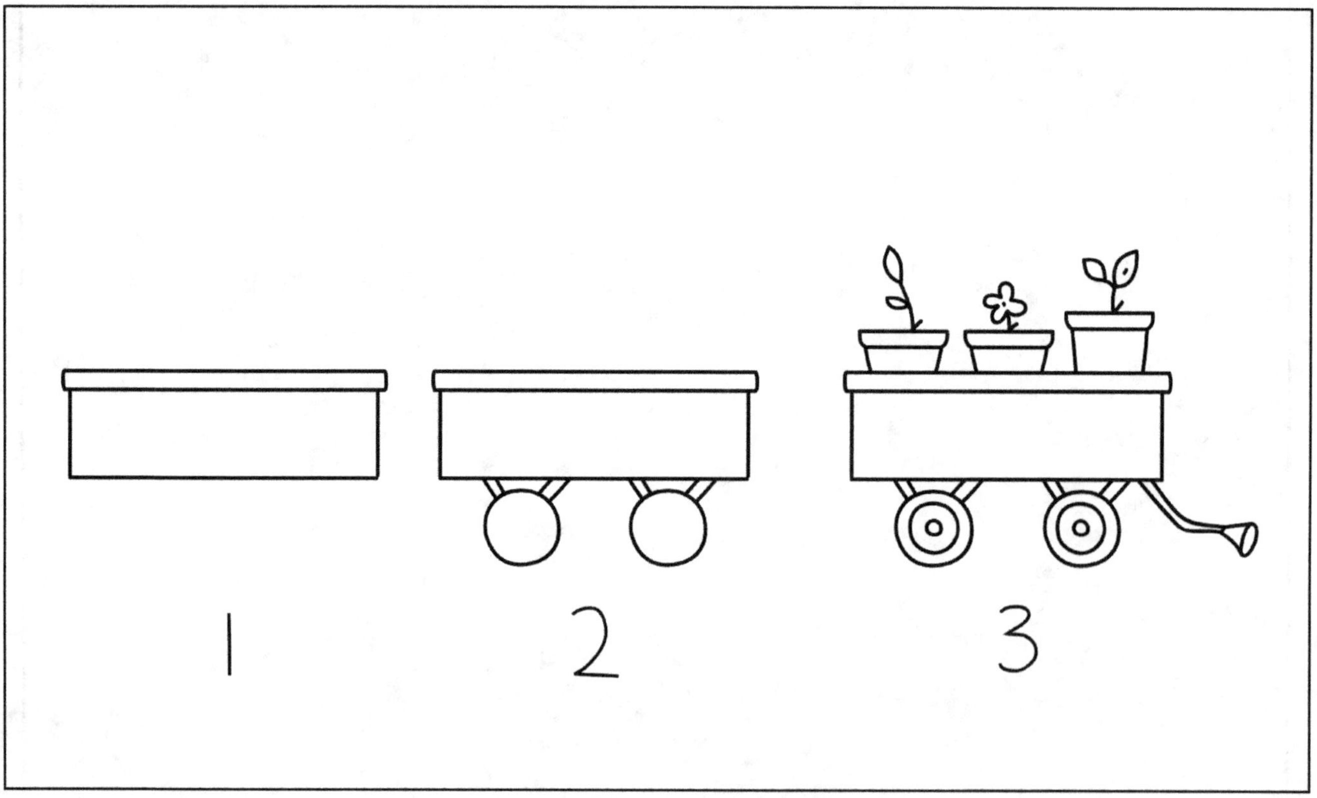

1

2

3

your turn to draw

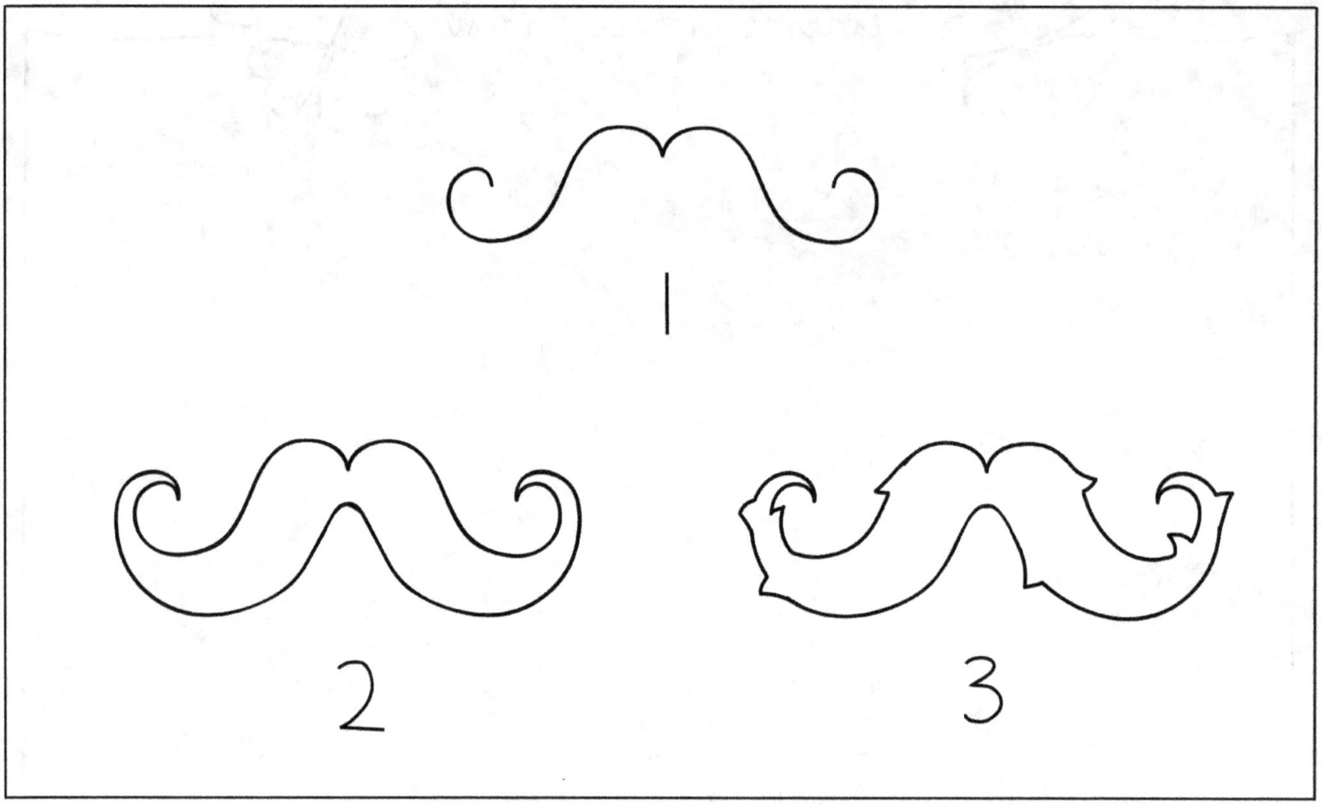

1

2

3

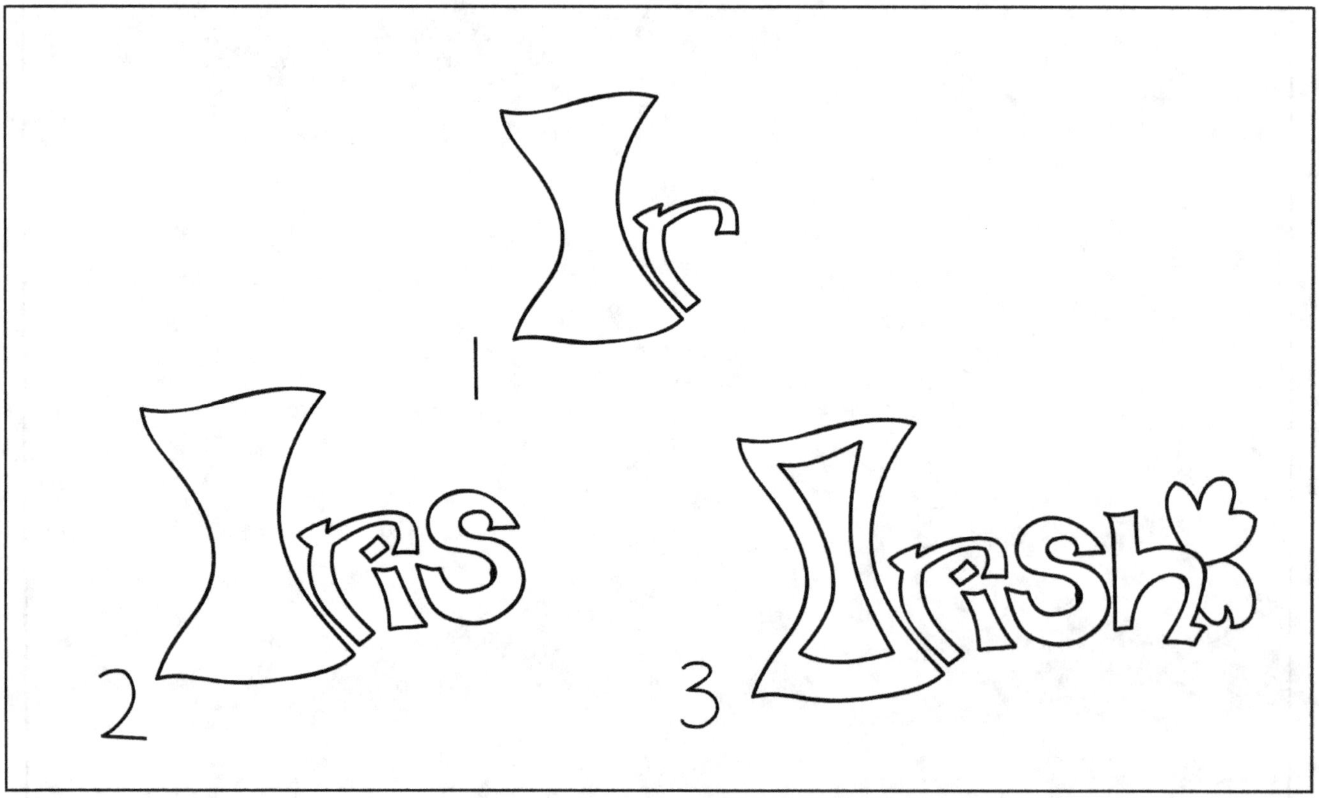

1

2

3

your turn to draw

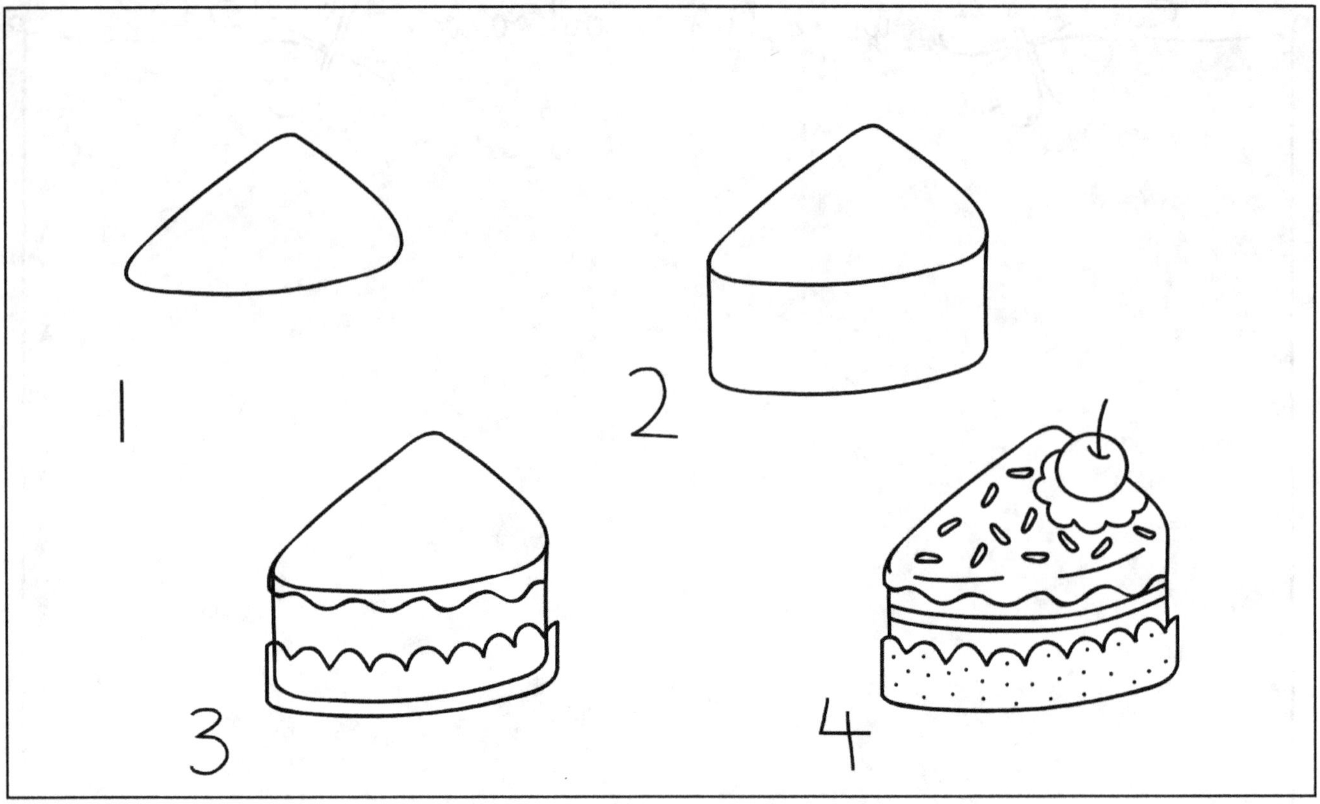

1

2

3

4

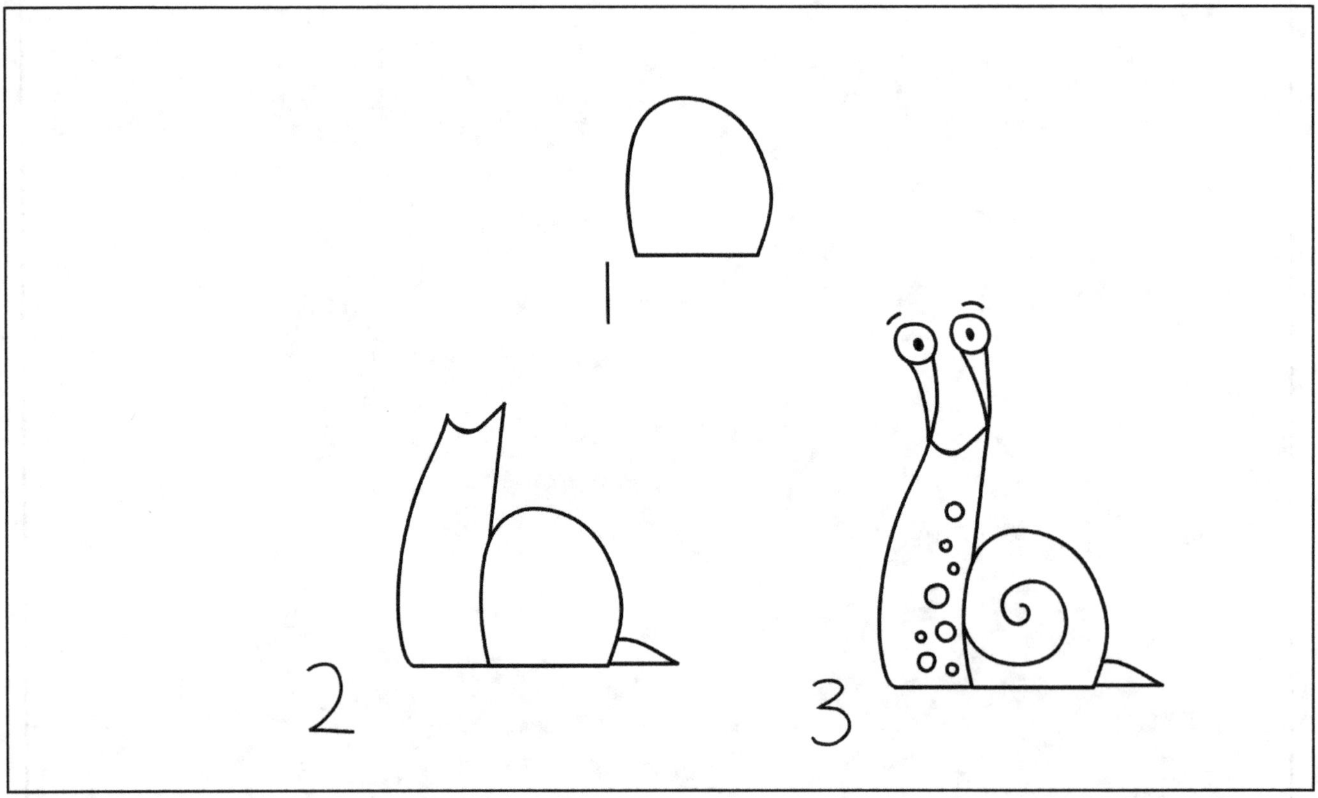

1

2

3

your turn to draw

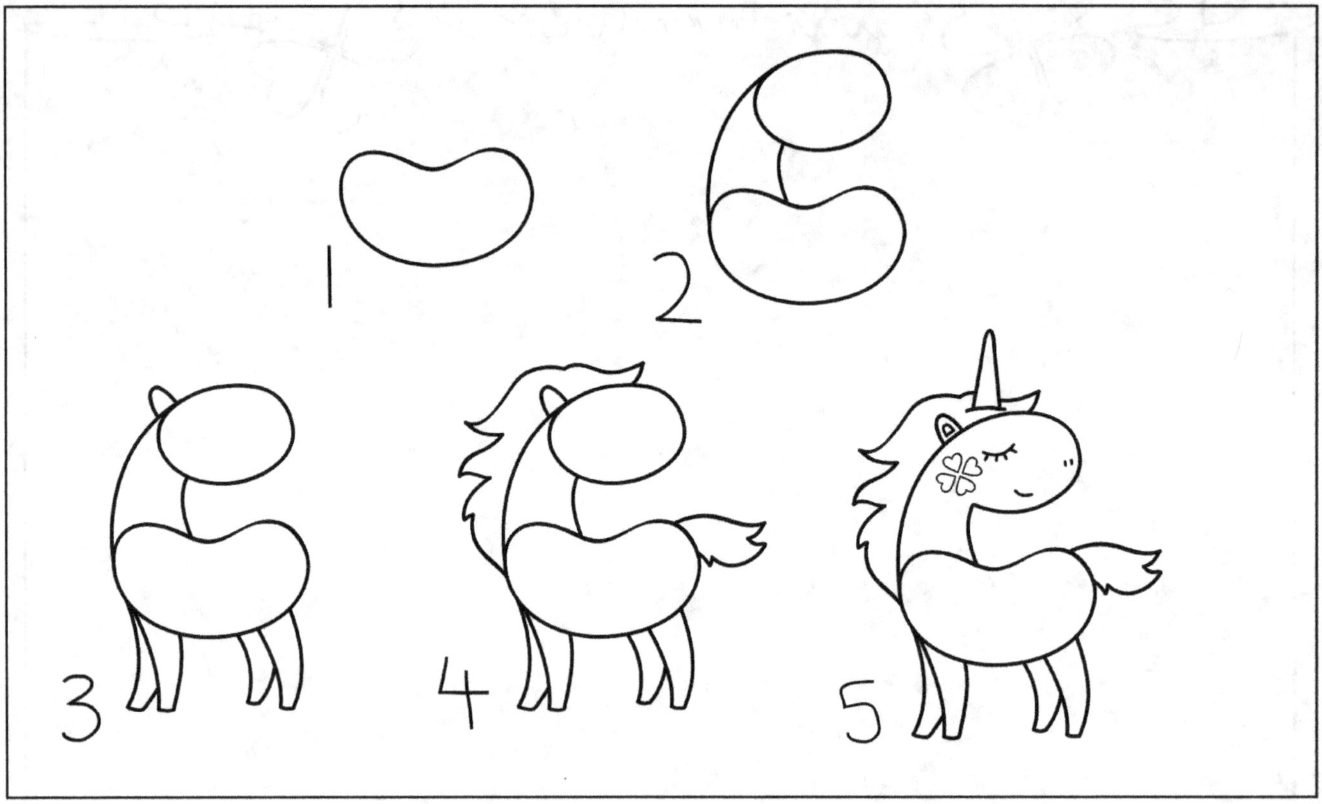

1

2

3

4

5

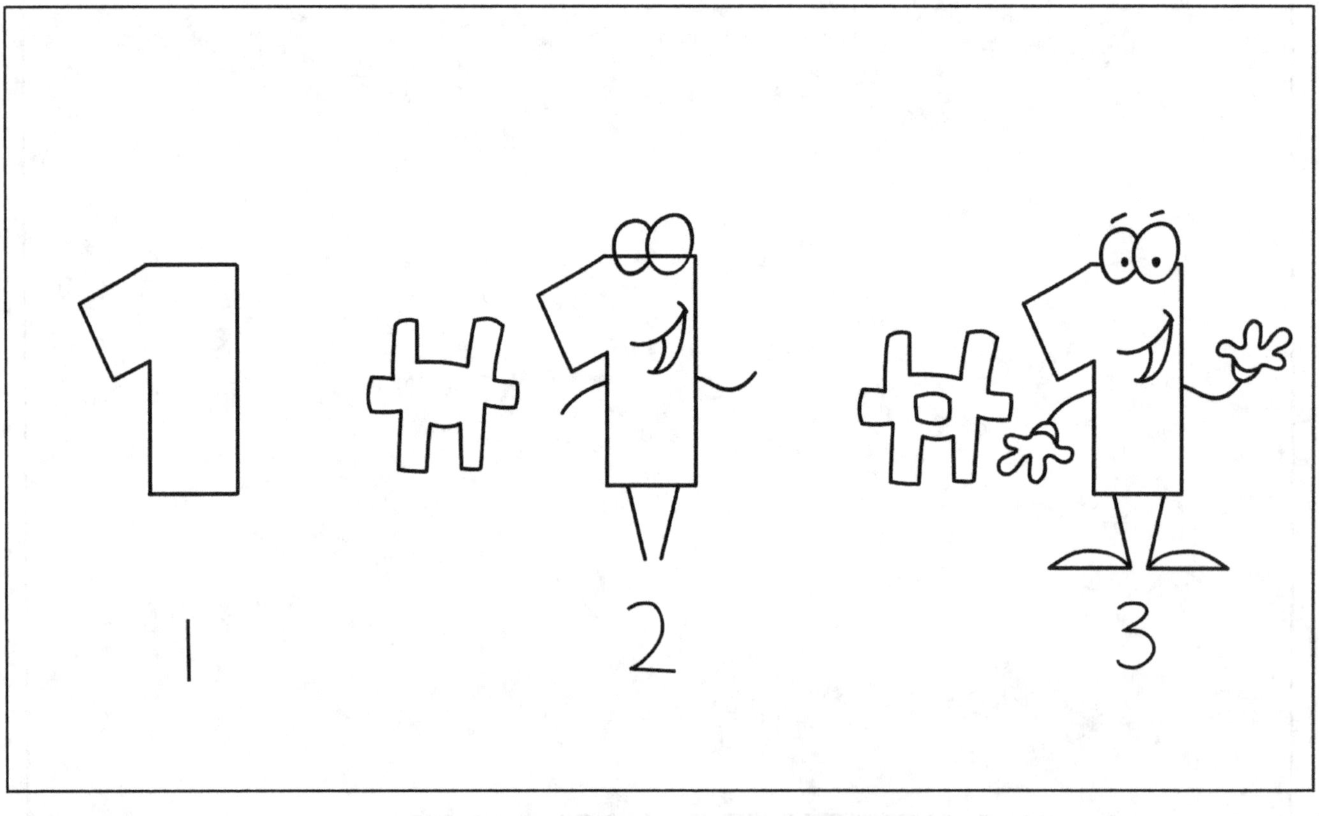

1

2

3

your turn to draw

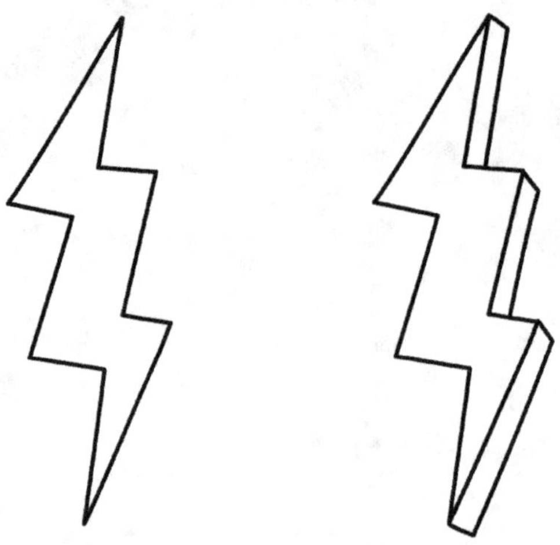

1   2   3

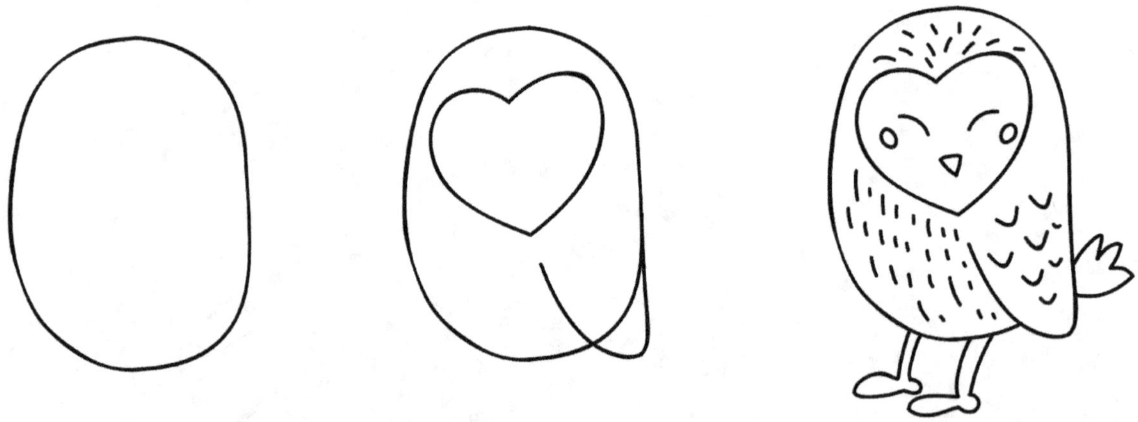

1   2   3

your turn to draw

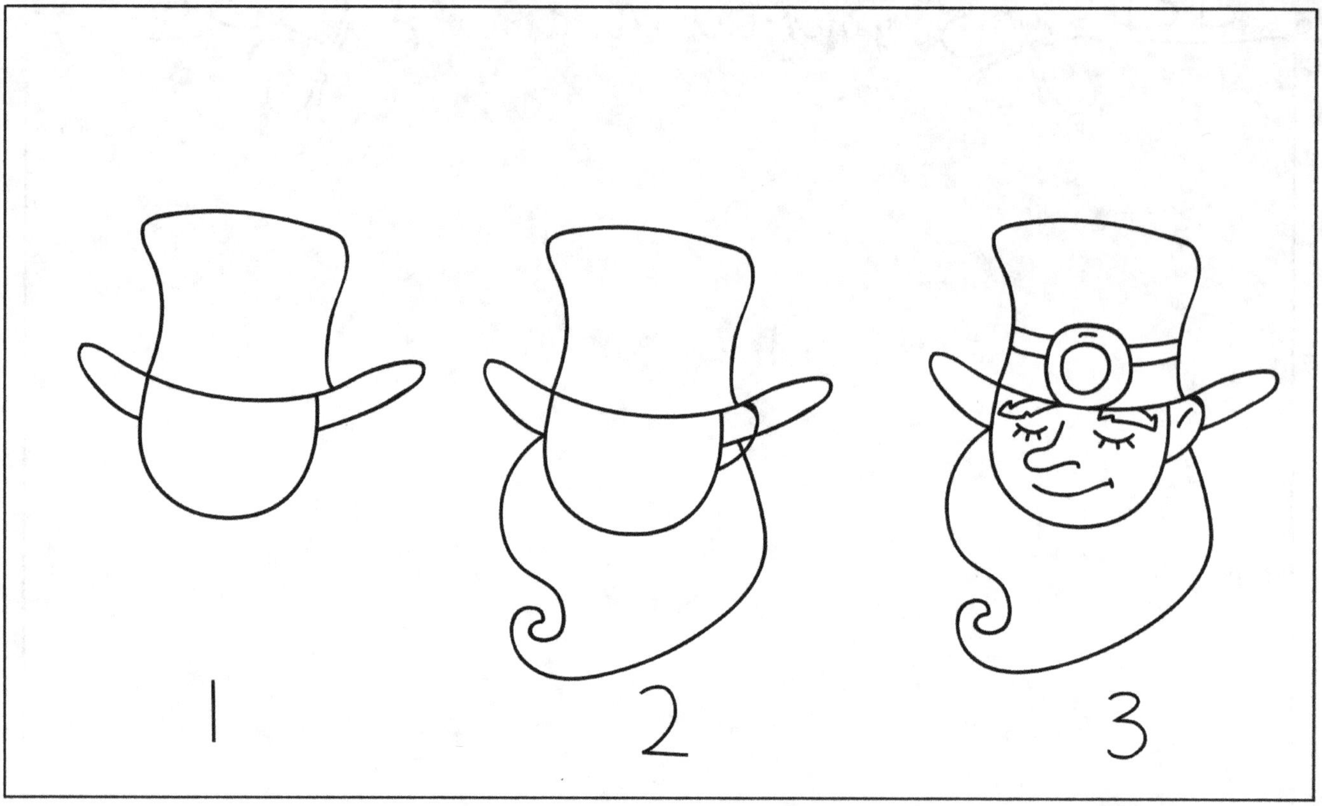

1

2

3

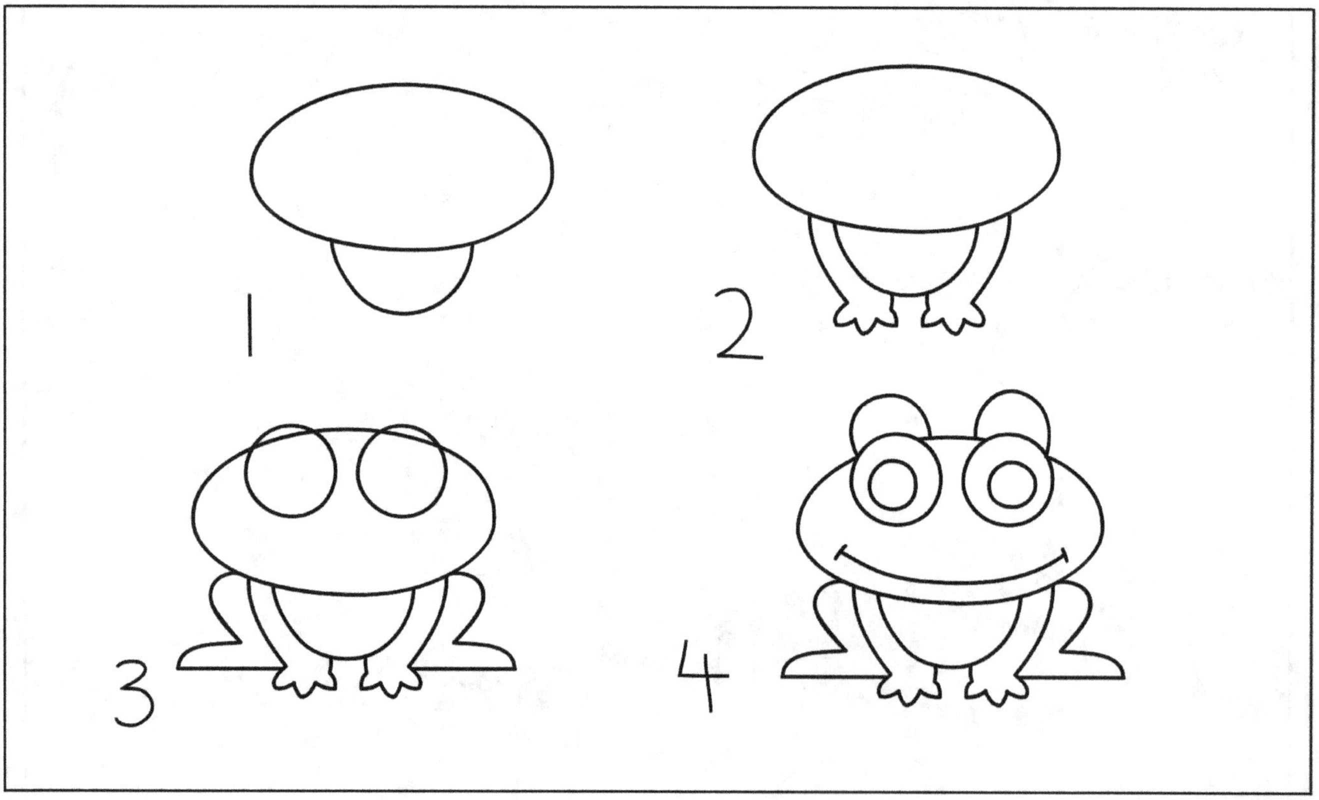

1

2

3

4

your turn to draw

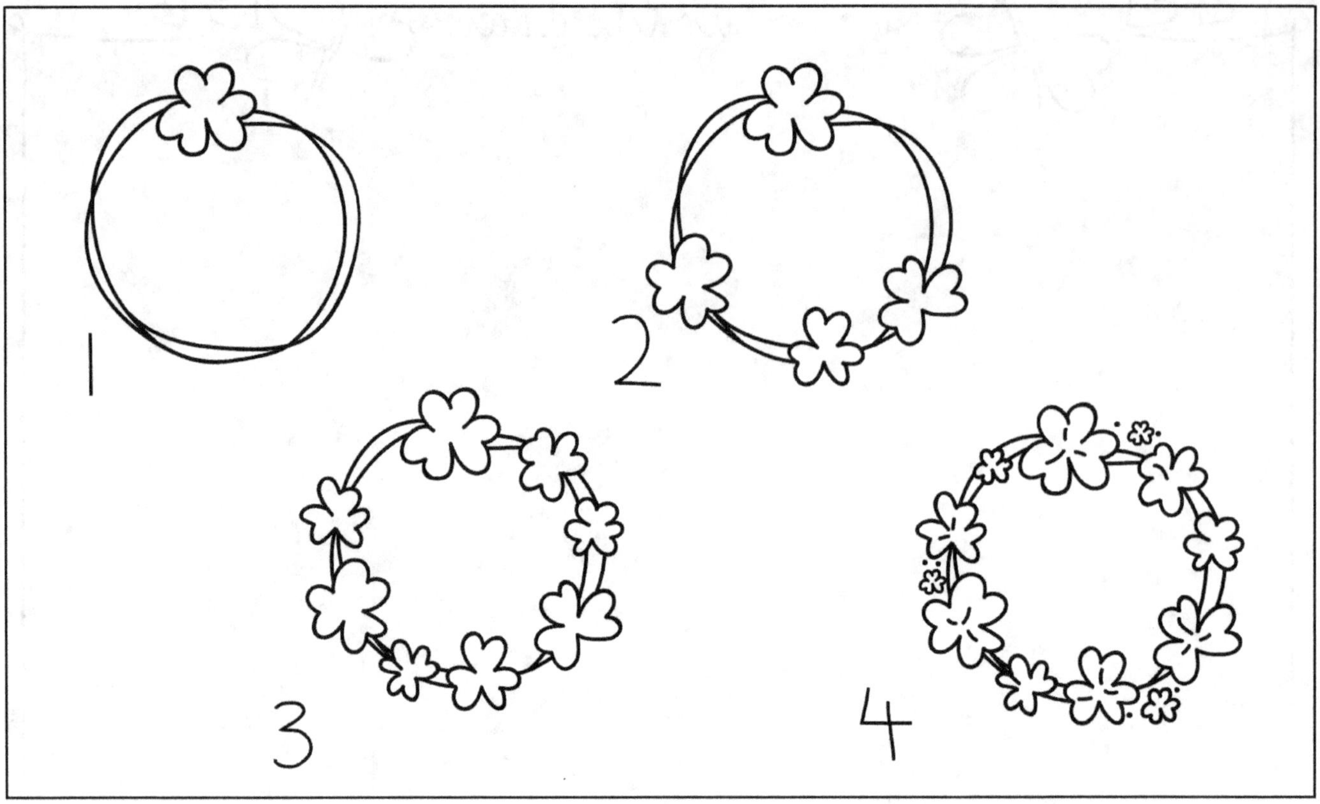

1

2

3

4

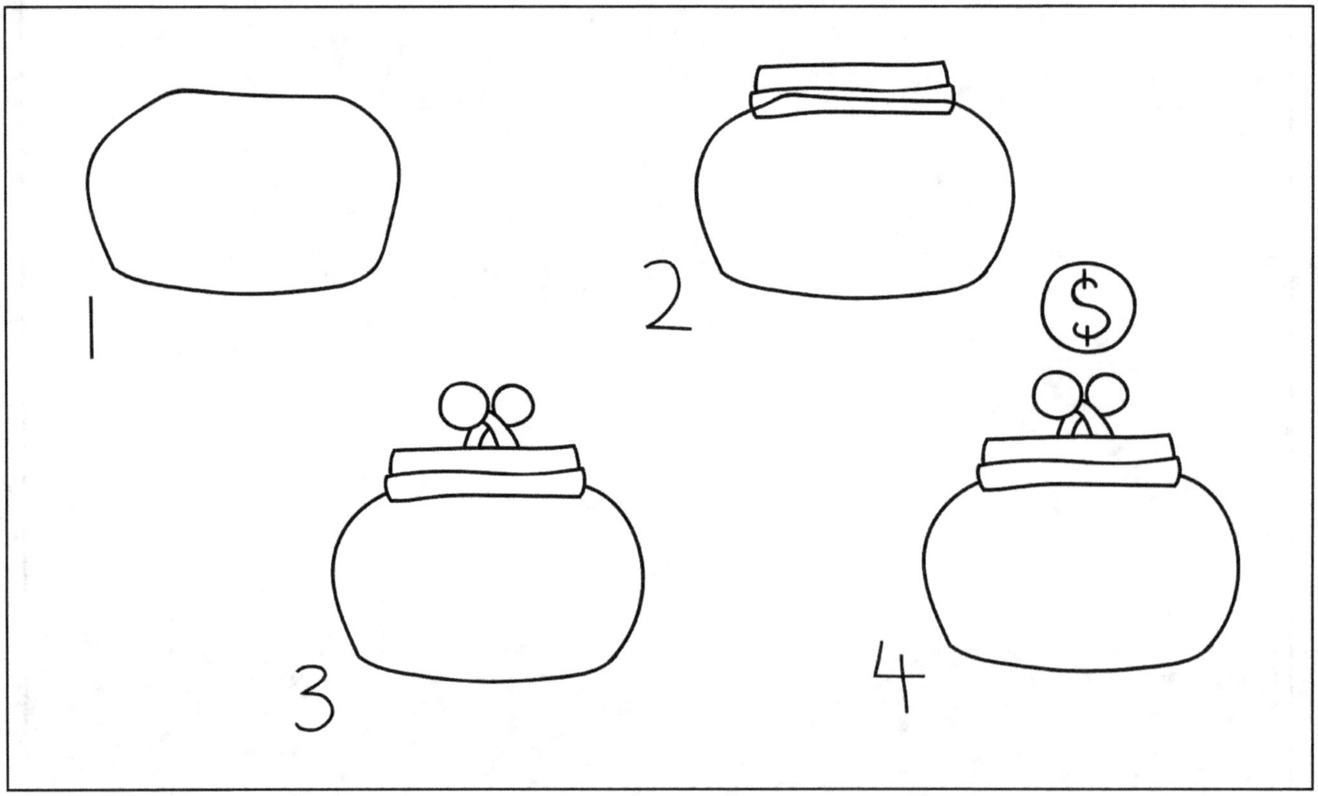

1

2

3

4

your turn to draw

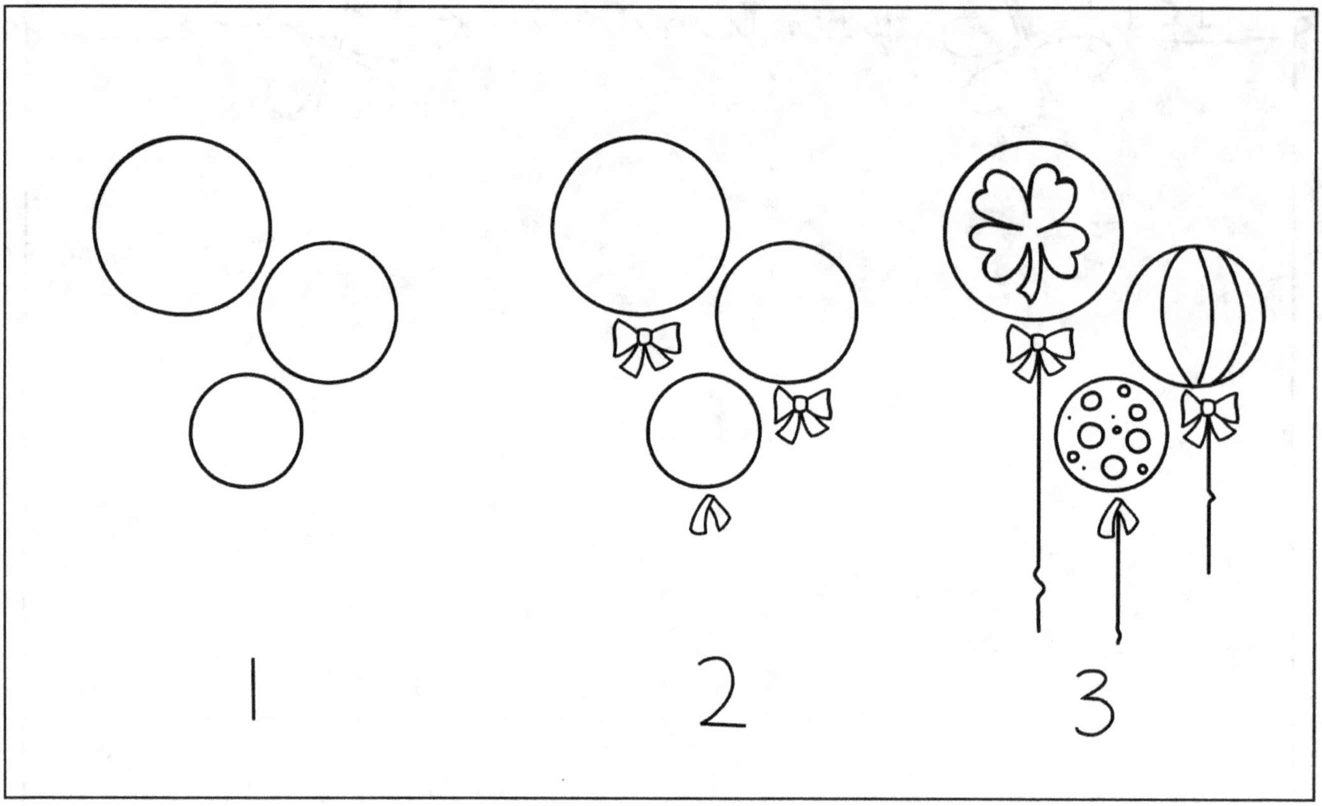

1

2

3

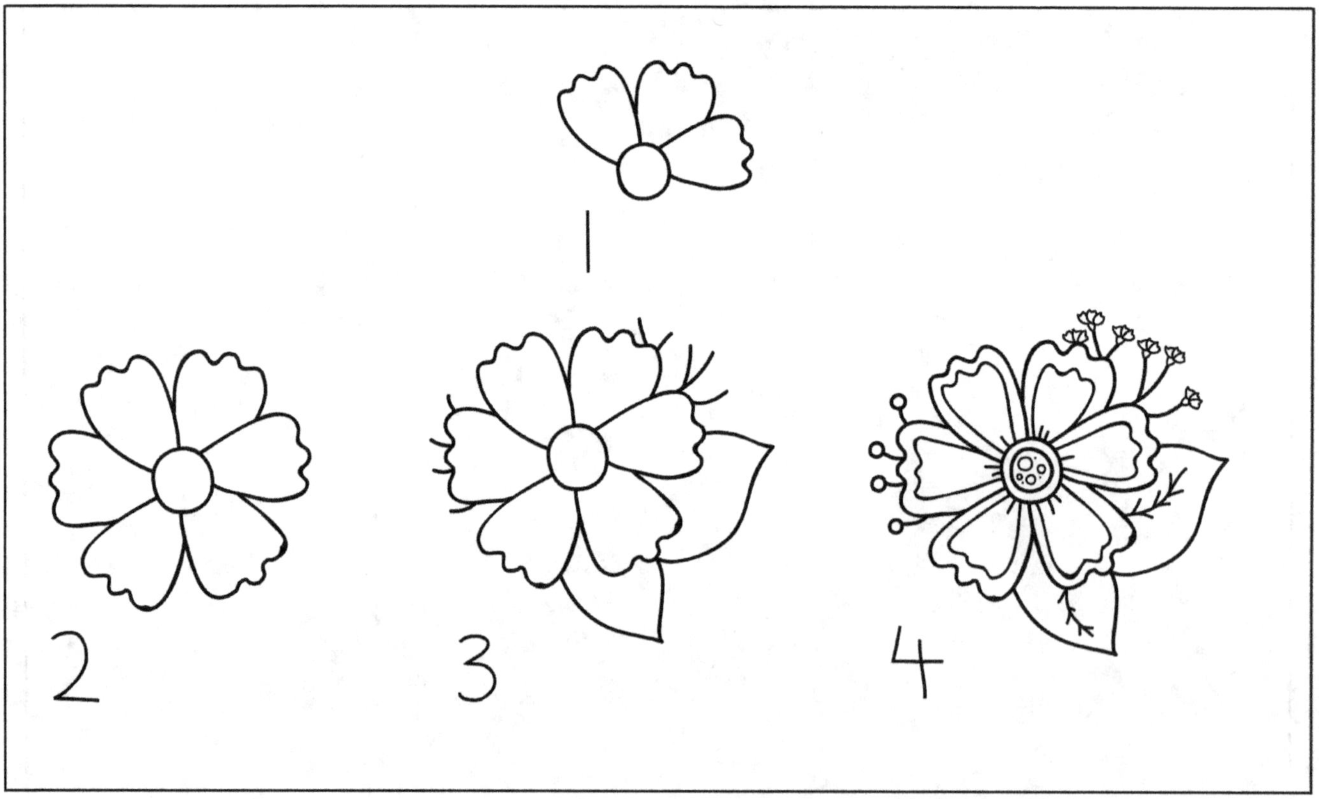

1

2

3

4

your turn to draw

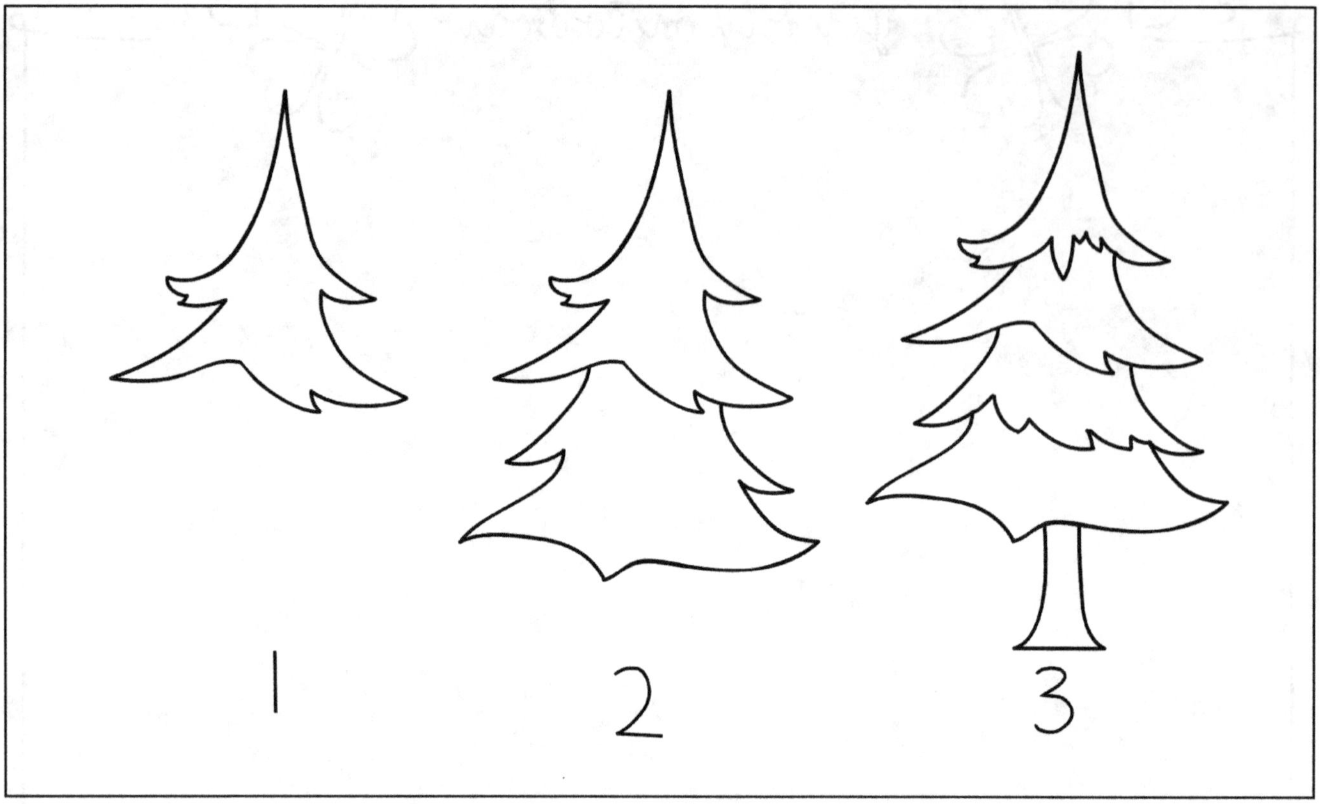

1

2

3

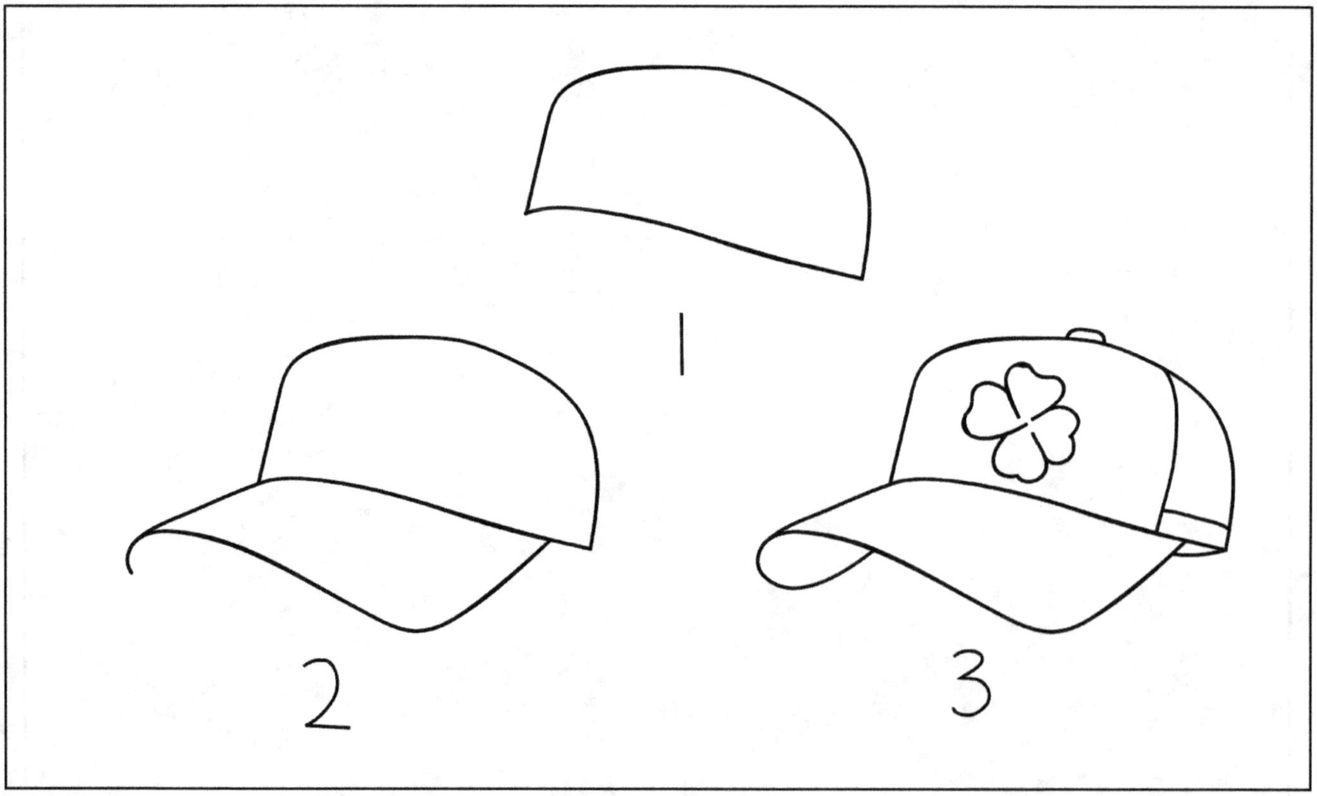

1

2

3

your turn to draw

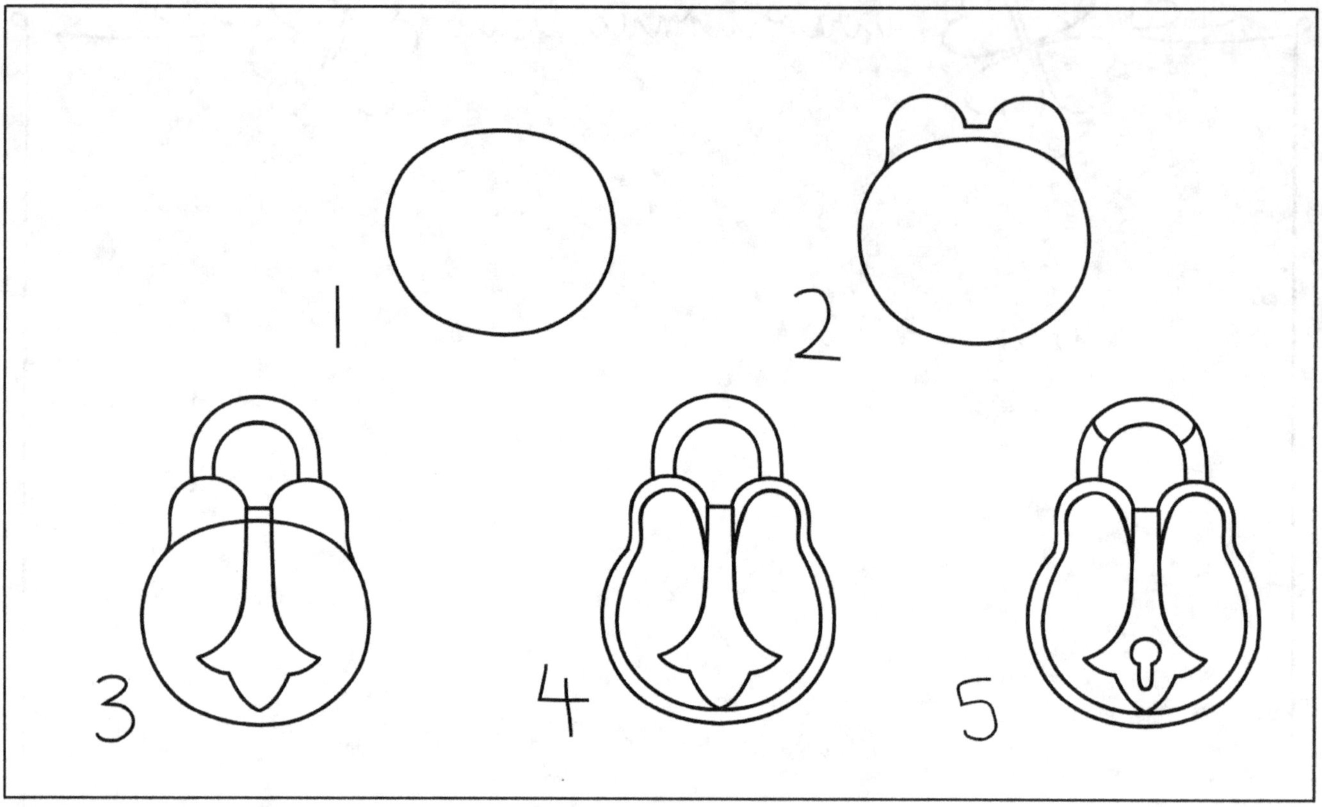

1

2

3

4

5

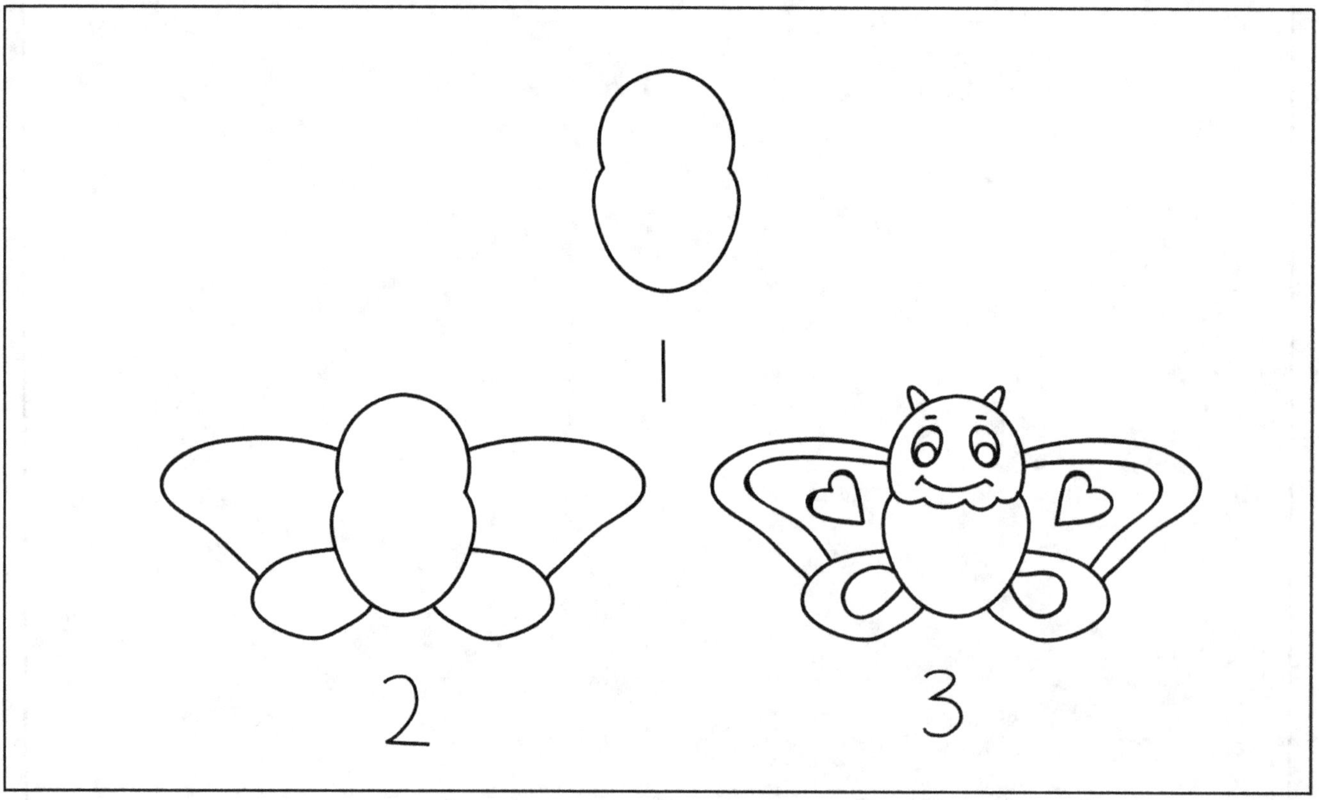

1

2

3

your turn to draw

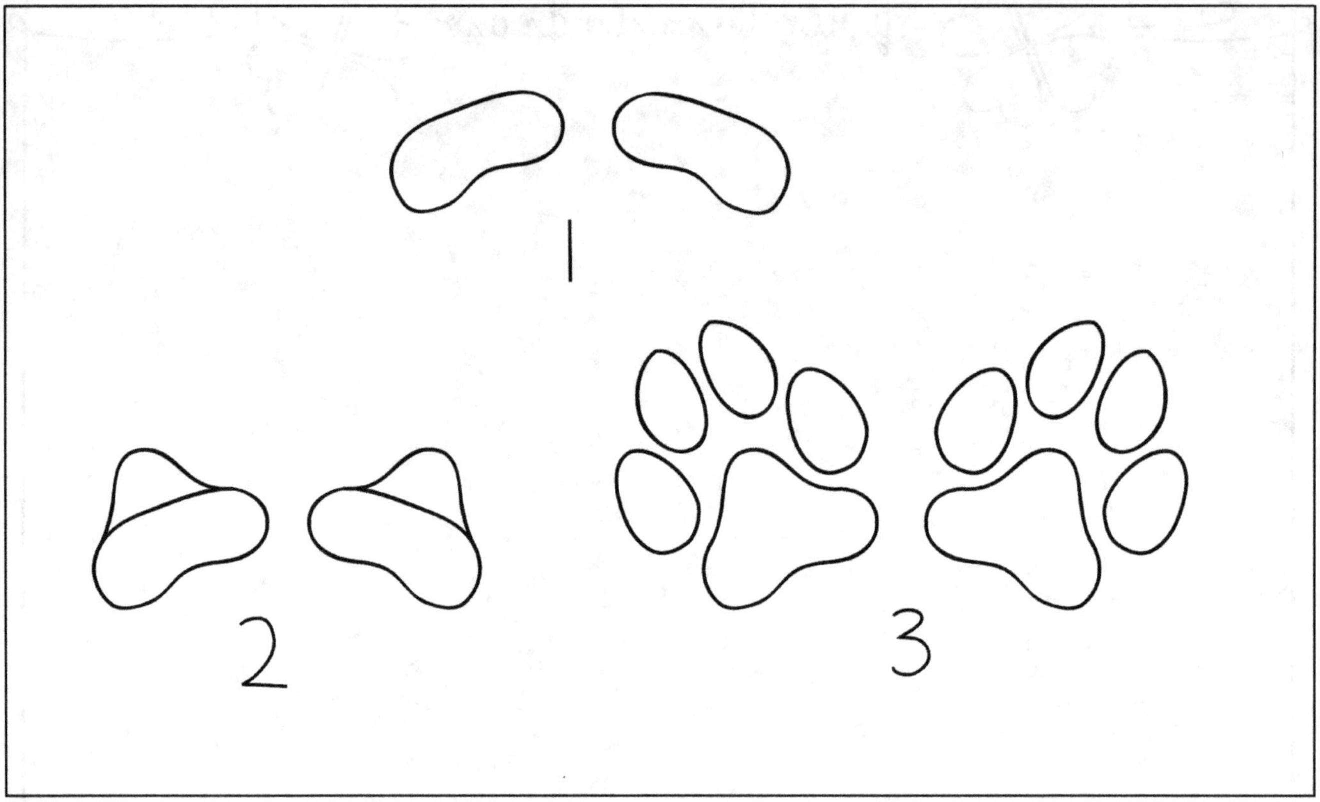

1

2

3

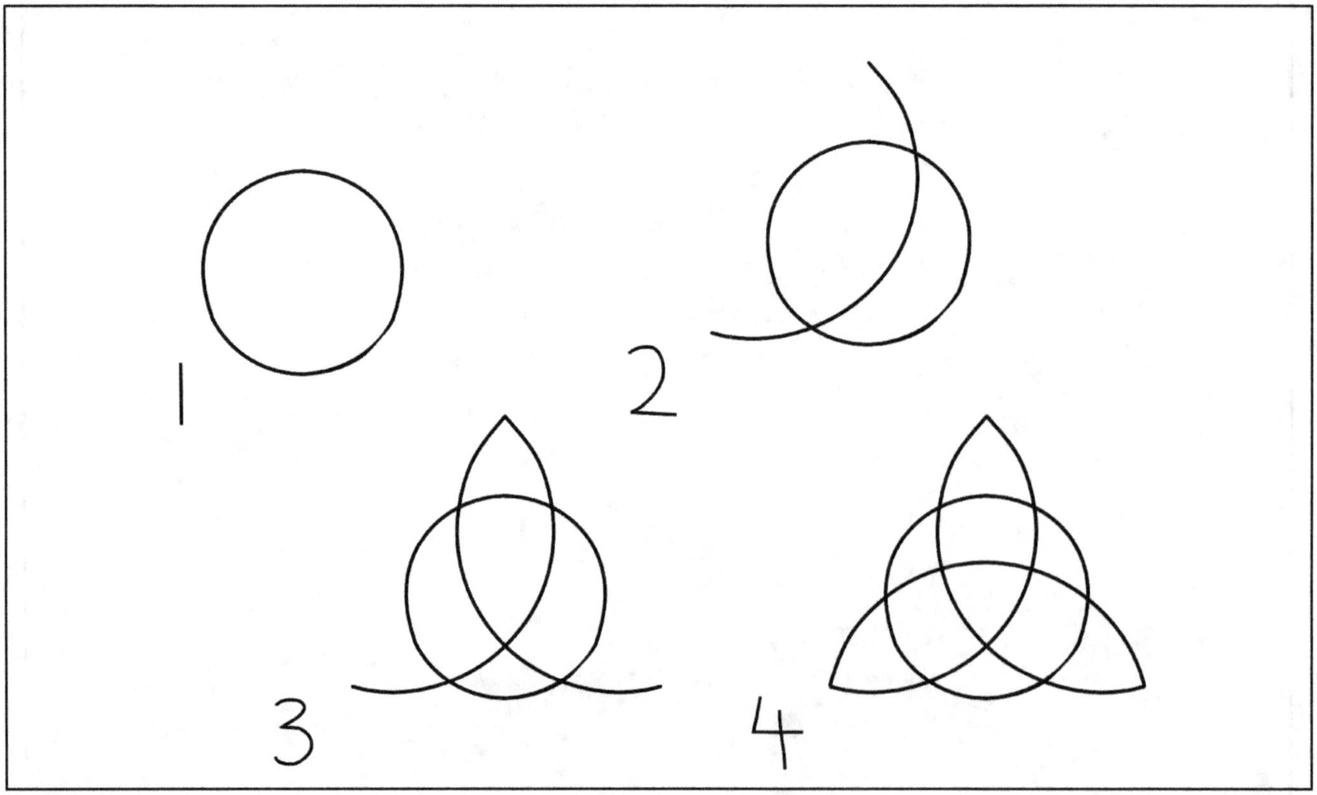

1

2

3

4

your turn to draw

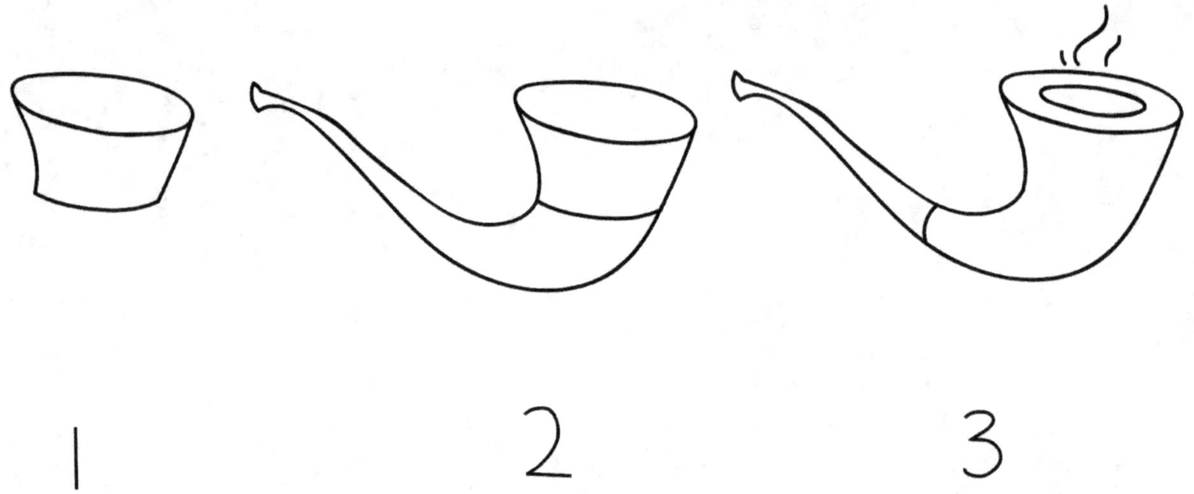

1   2   3

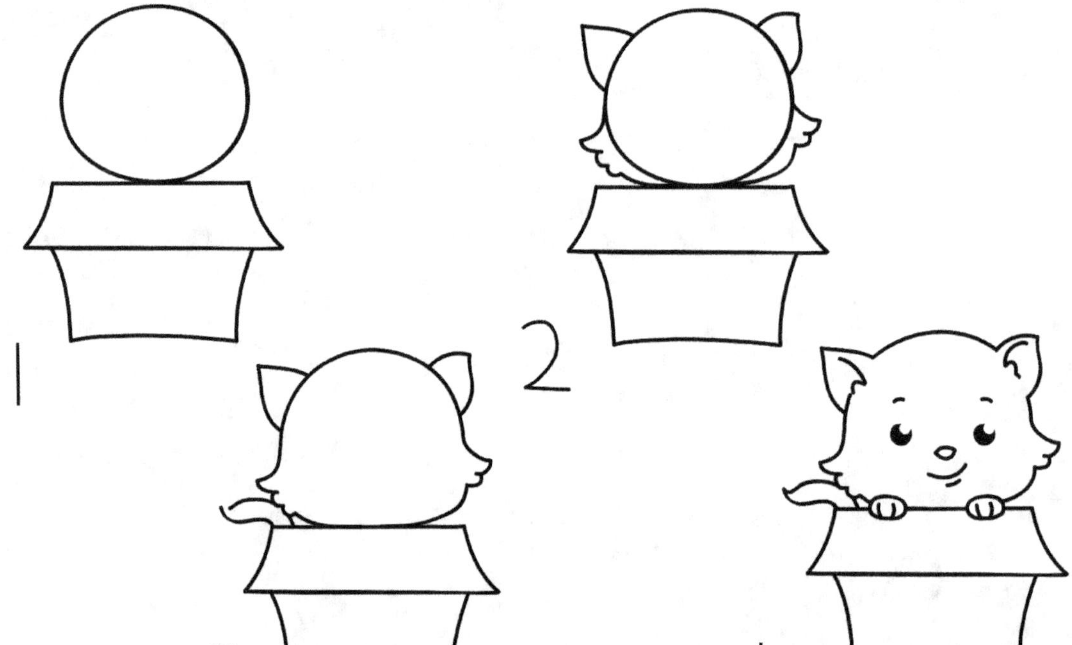

1   2   3   4

your turn to draw

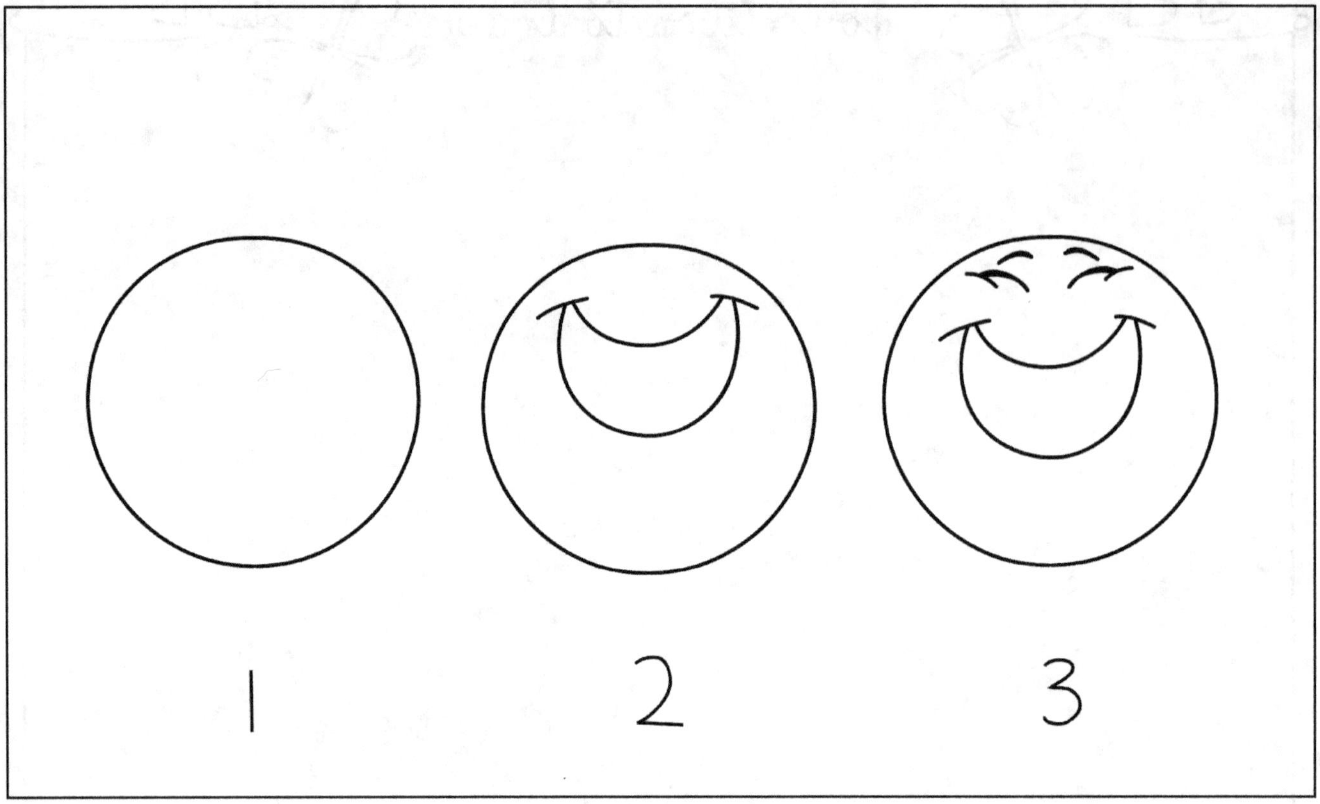

1   2   3

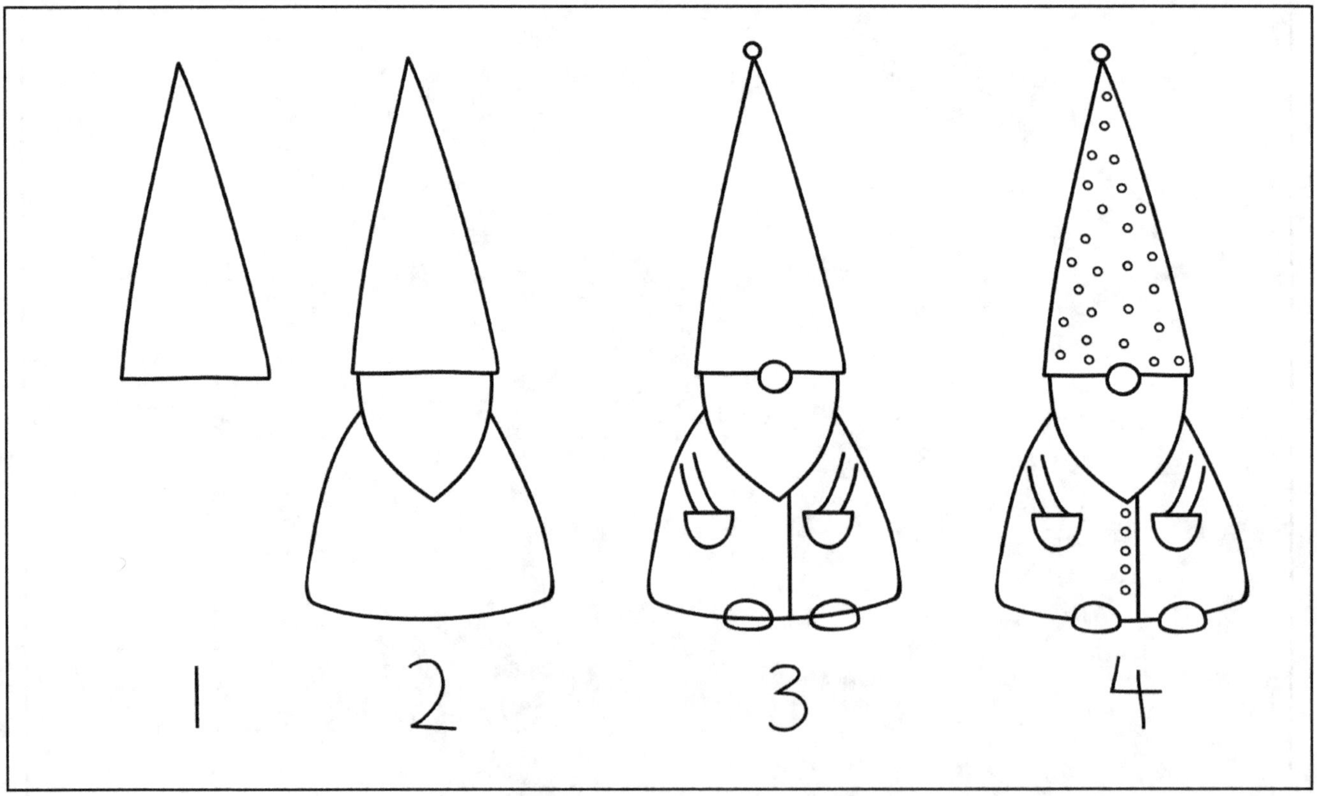

1   2   3   4

your turn to draw

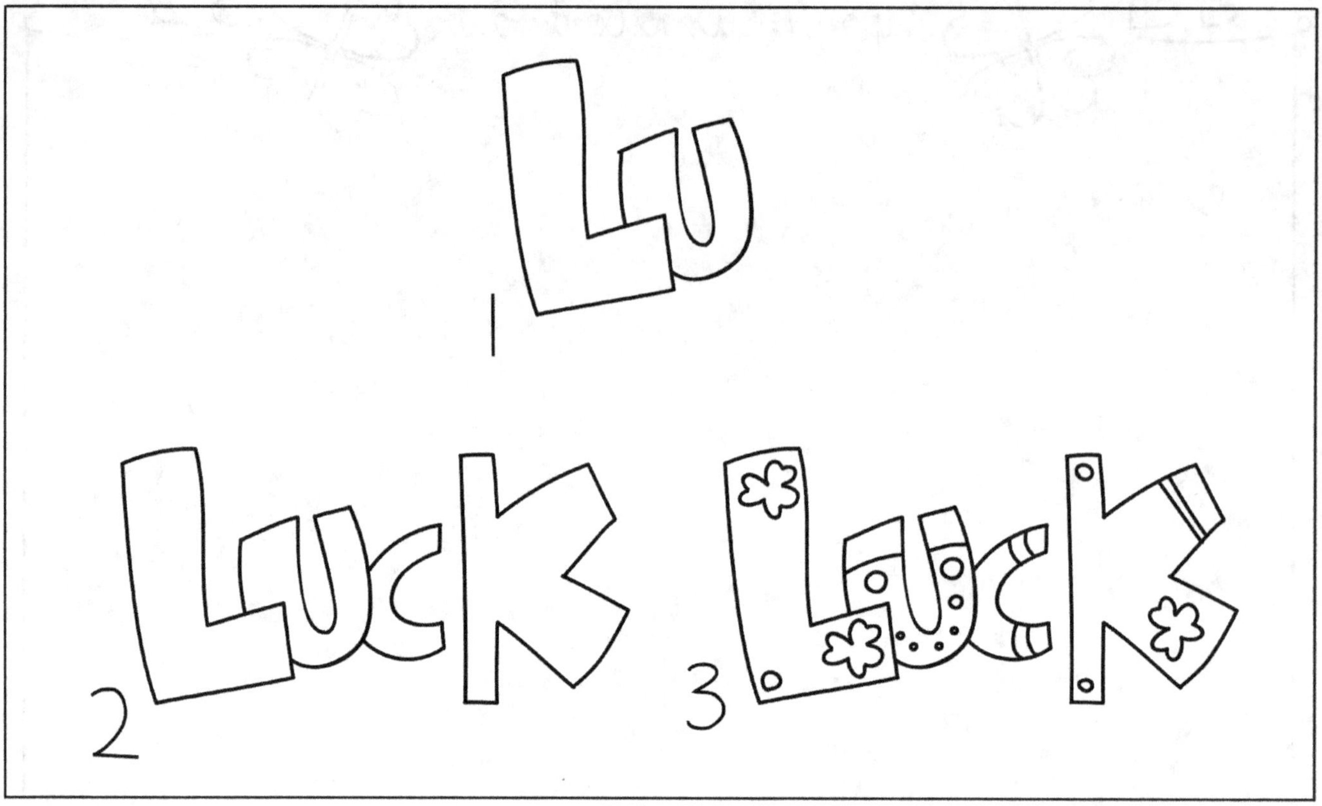

LU

1

LUCK

2

LUCK

3

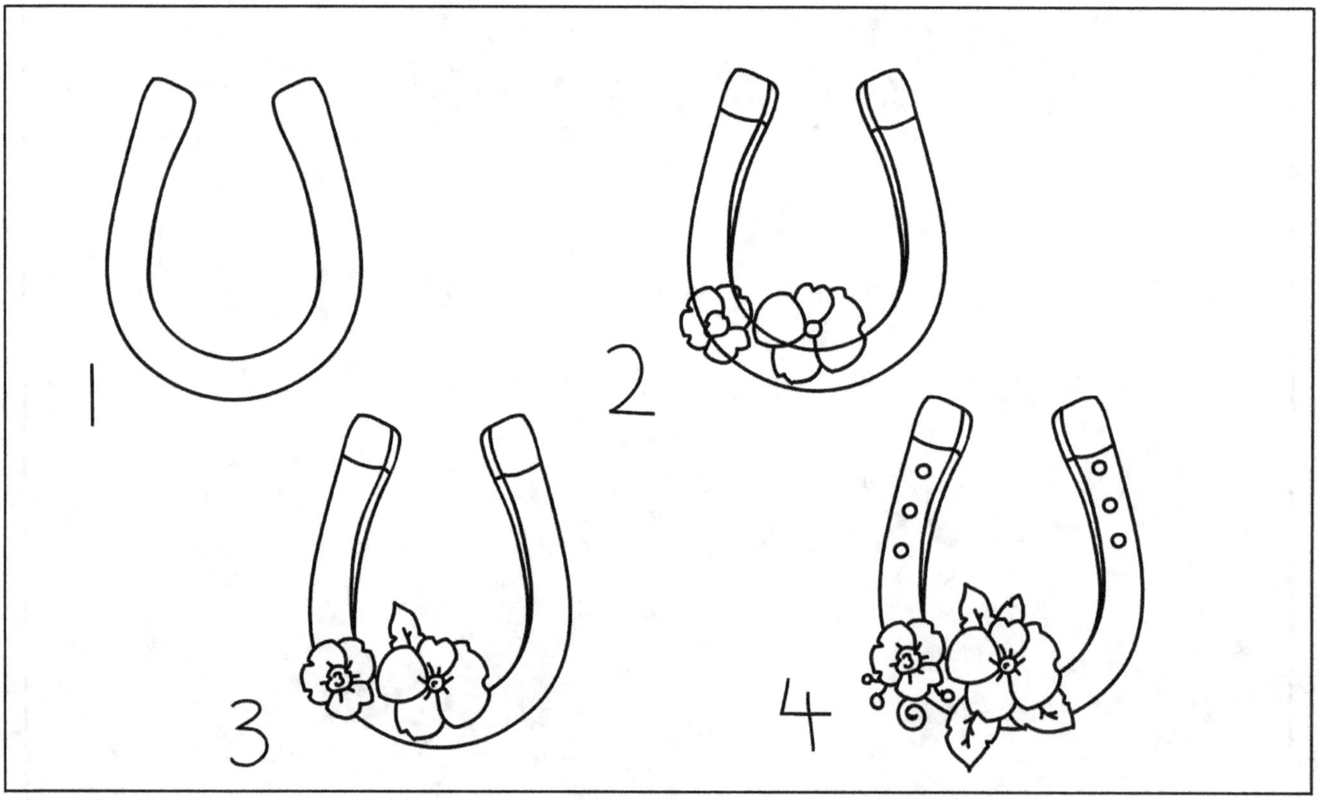

1

2

3

4

your turn to draw

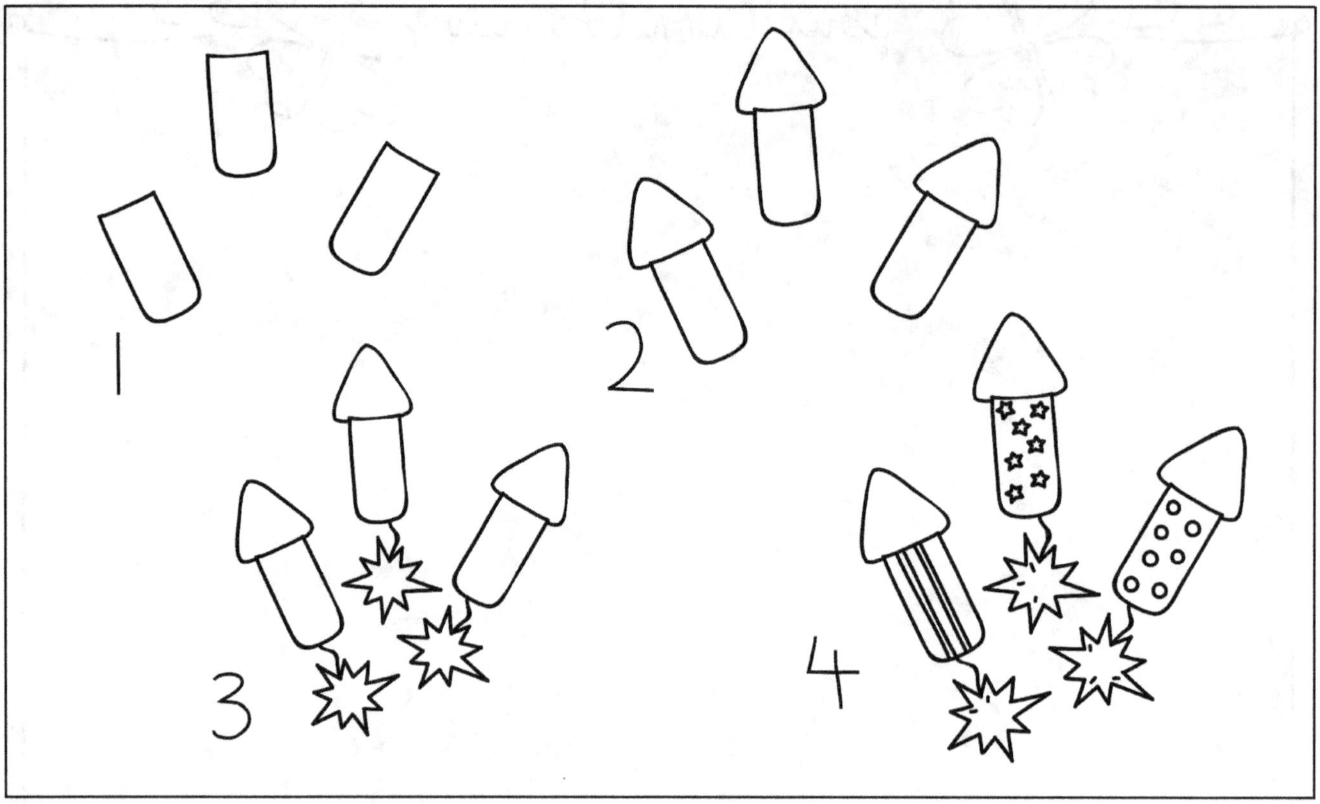

1

2

3

4

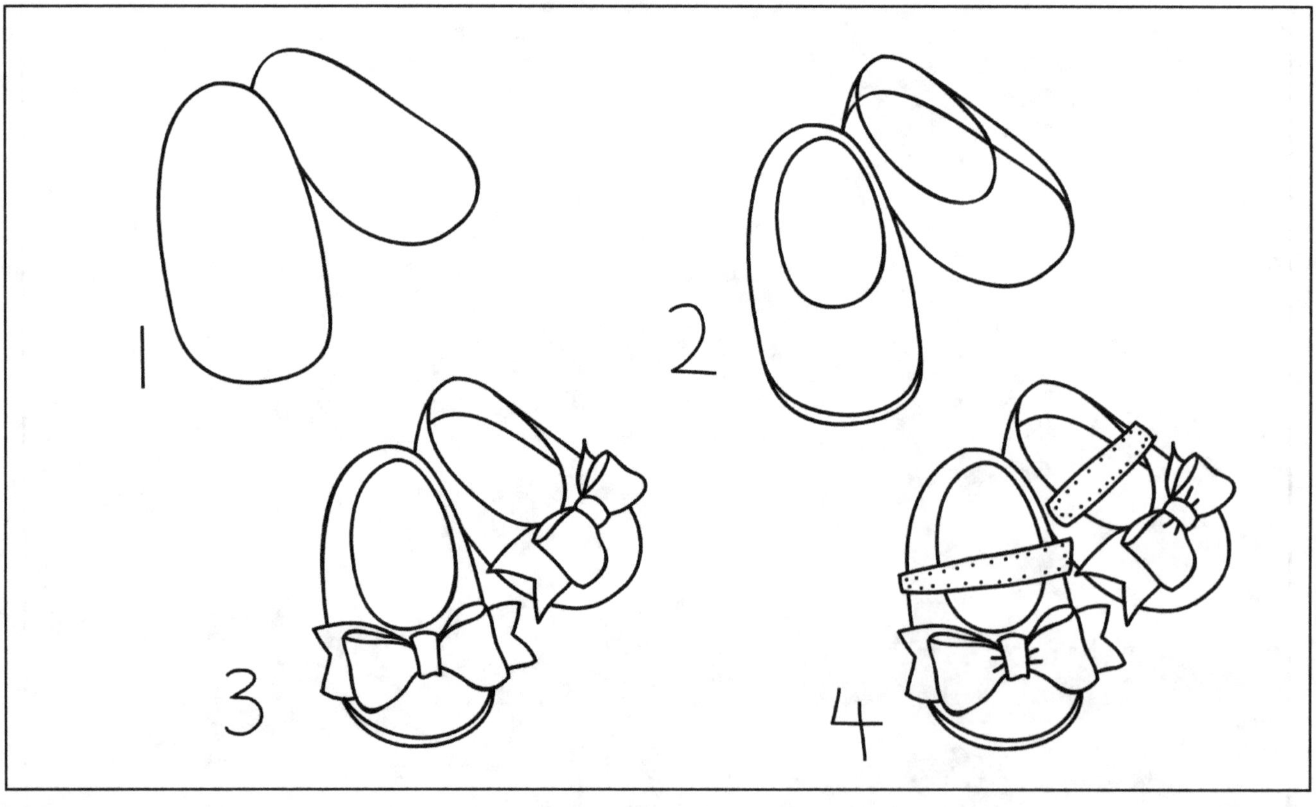

1

2

3

4

your turn to draw

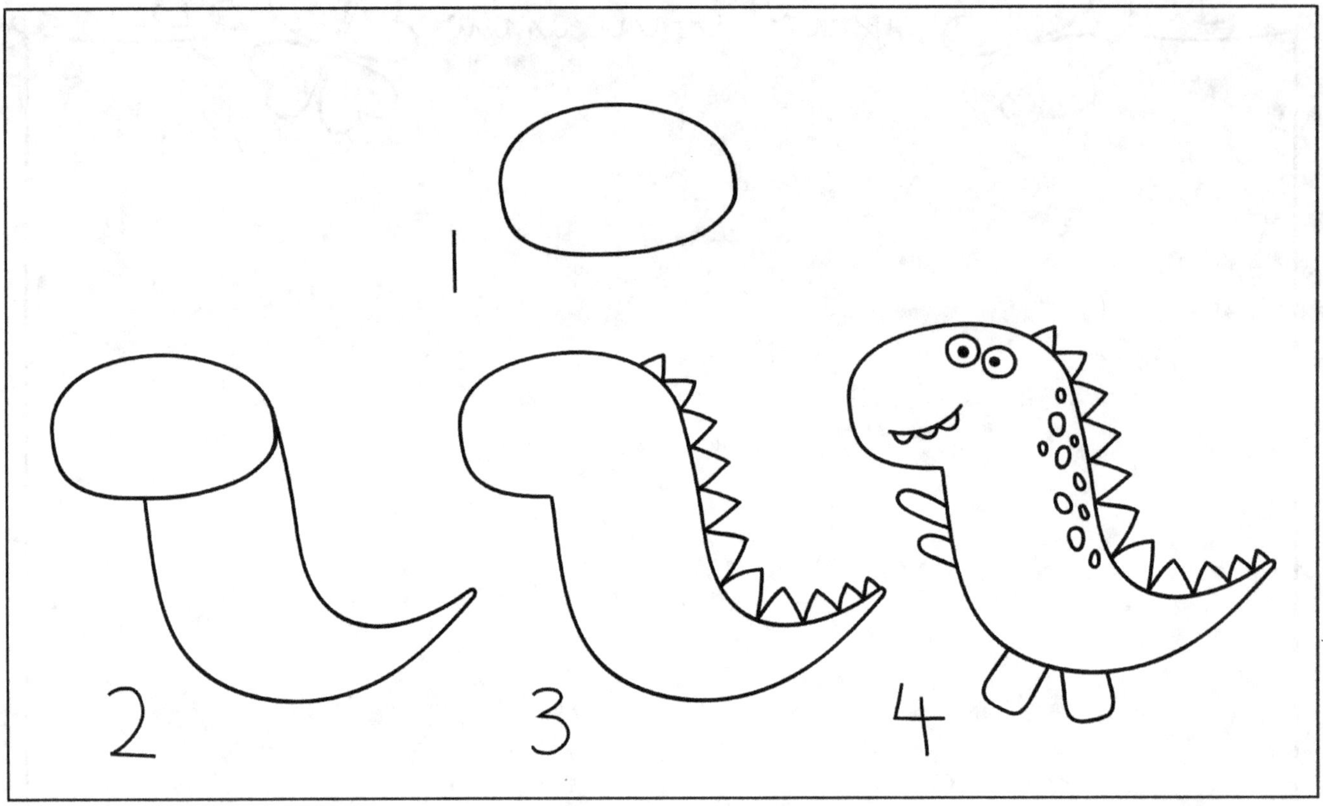

1

2   3   4

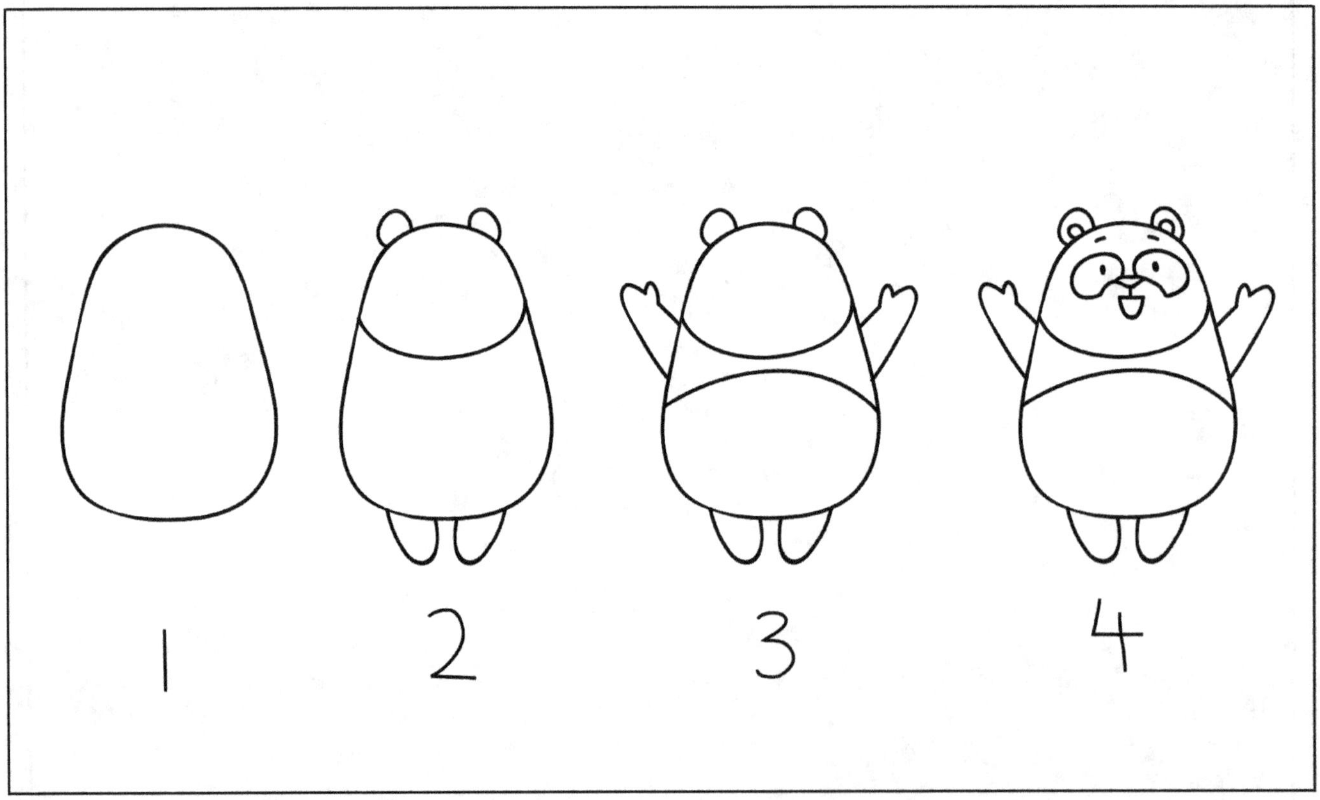

1   2   3   4

your turn to draw

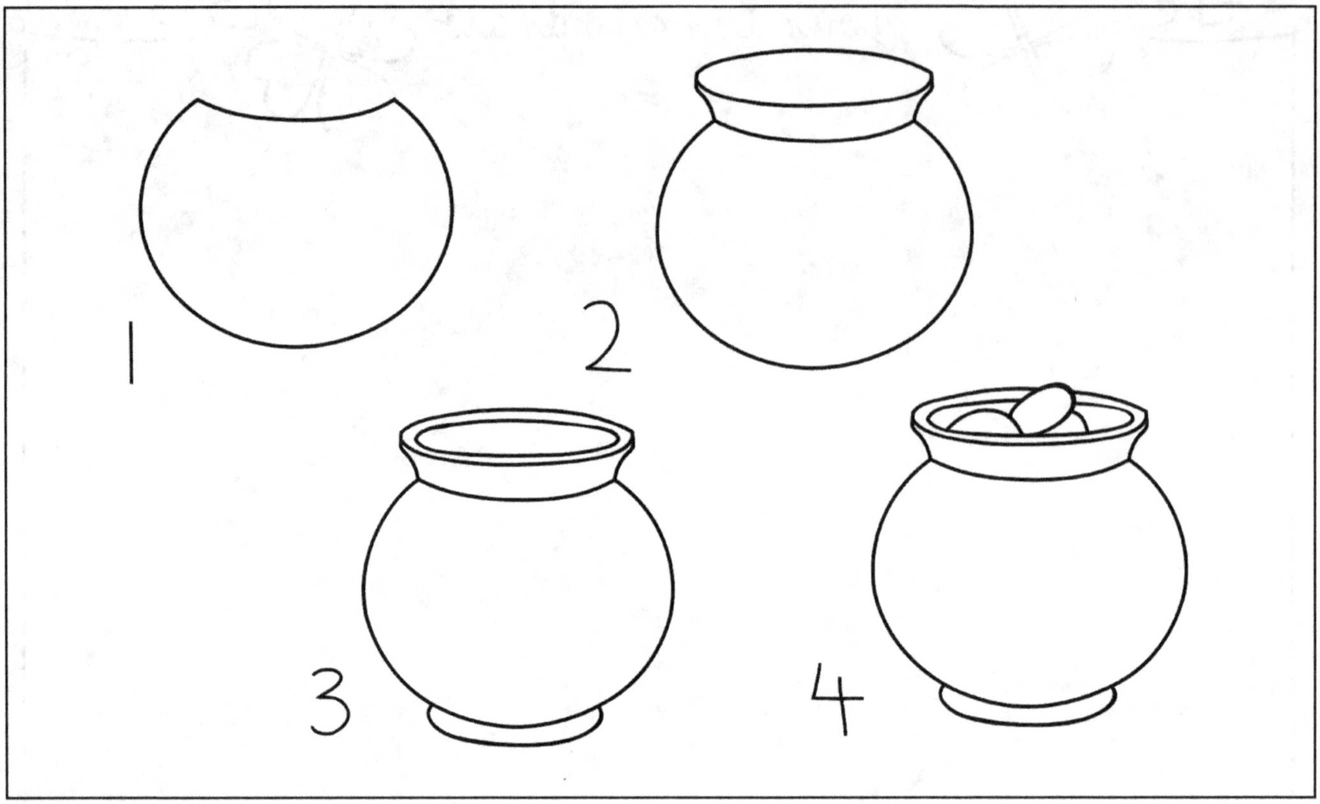

1

2

3

4

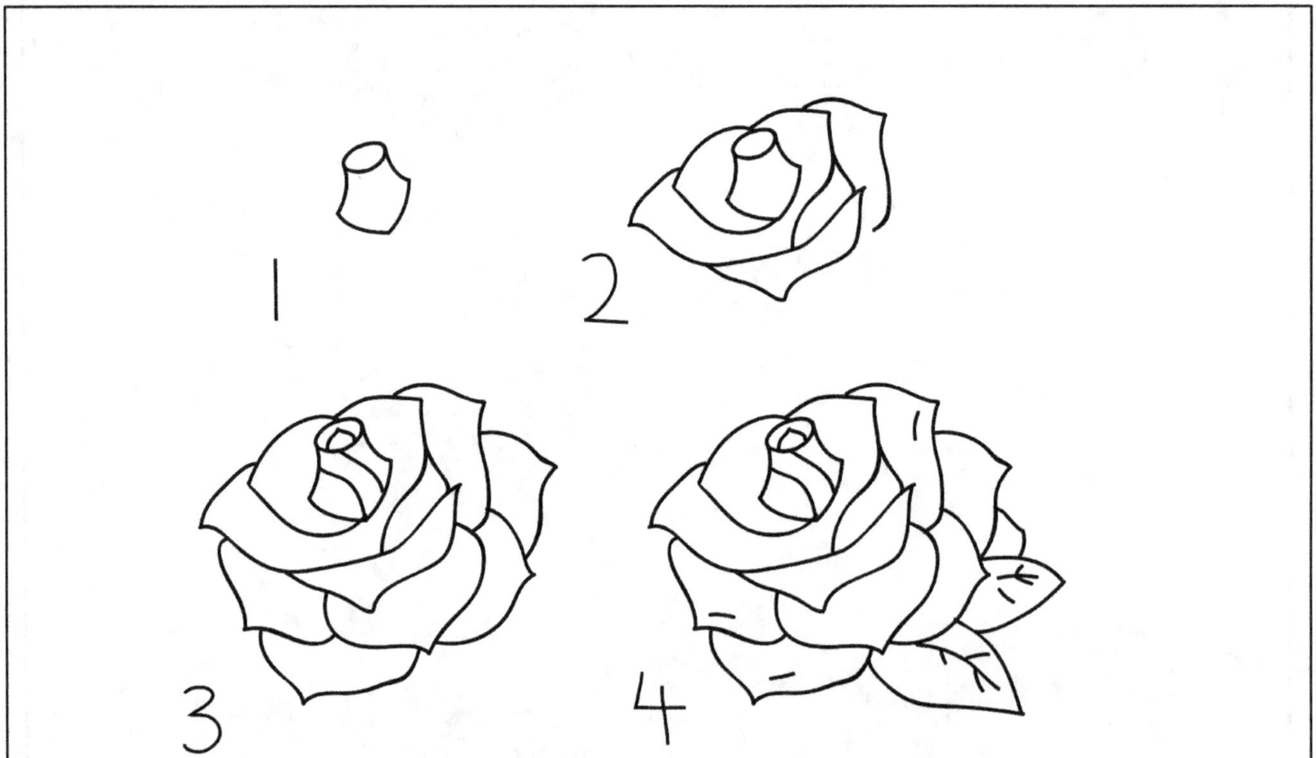

1

2

3

4

your turn to draw

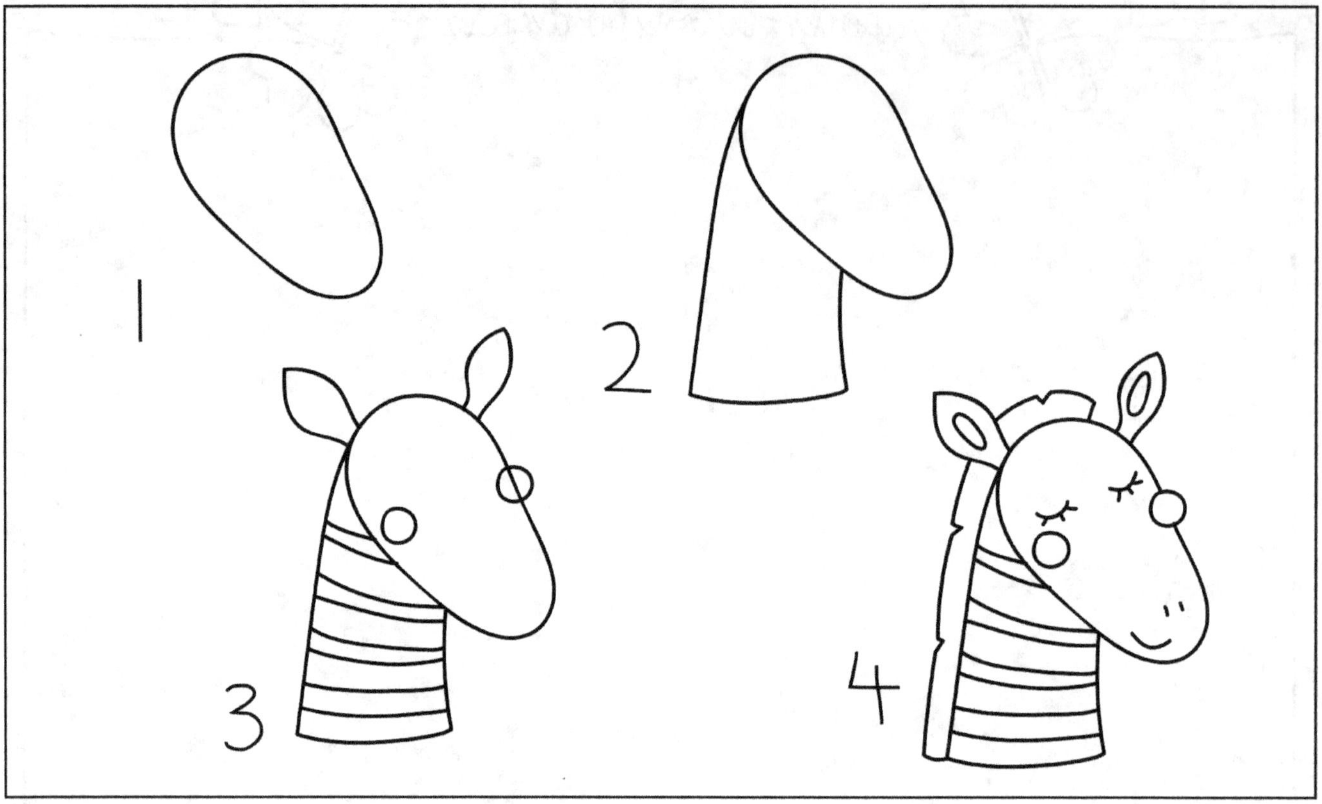

1

2

3

4

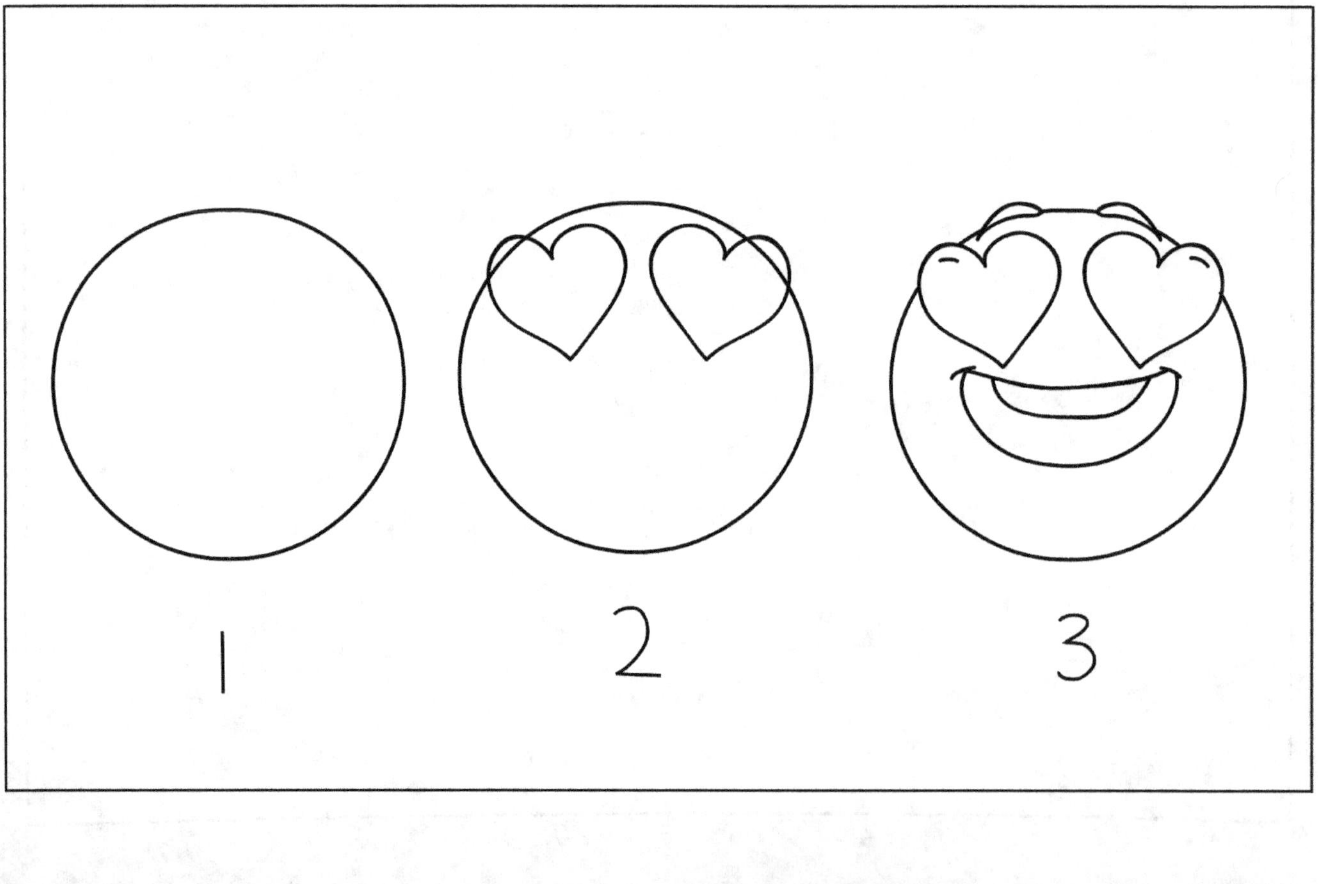

1

2

3

your turn to draw

www.ingramcontent.com/pod-product-compliance
Lightning Source LLC
Chambersburg PA
CBHW081610220526
45468CB00010B/2835